POWER

AND

MORALITY

WHO SHALL GUARD THE GUARDIANS?

POWER AND MORALITY

WHO SHALL GUARD THE GUARDIANS?

By

PITIRIM A. SOROKIN

WALTER A. LUNDEN

leksandrovich

AN EXTENDING HORIZONS BOOK

PORTER SARGENT PUBLISHER

Boston 8, Massachusetts

Copyright 1959

by

F. Porter Sargent

THE AUTHORS

PITIRIM A. SOROKIN was born and spent his childhood among the Komi, Ugri-Finnish people north of Russia. Up to his eleventh year, he had not seen a town nor learned to read or write. Orphaned at 10, and self-taught, he then became a student of a teachers college, was arrested and imprisoned for his political activities in 1906, then became "a starving and hunted revolutionary", and a student of a night school, of the Psycho-Neurological Institute, and of the University of St. Petersburg. Two more imprisonments gave him a first-hand experience in criminology, the field of his graduate study and then of his first professorship. He published his first volume, *Crime and Punishment: Service and Reward*, in 1913, and three years later received the Magister's degree in criminal law, and in 1922 the degree of Doctor of Sociology from the University of St. Petersburg.

With the explosion of the Russian Revolution, he became one of the founders of the Russian Peasant Soviet, which was dispersed by the Communists. From the beginning of the Revolution, he vigorously fought Lenin, Trotsky, Kamenev, and other communist leaders. Arrested January 3, 1918 and imprisoned for four months in the Fortress of Peter and Paul, he was then released, only to resume his struggle against the communists. In October of the same year, he was again arrested, was condemned to death, but by Lenin's order was freed and permitted to return to his academic activities at the University of St. Petersburg. There he became the founder, first professor, and chairman of the Department of Sociology; during the years 1920-1922 he published five volumes in law and sociology. In 1922, he was again arrested, this time to be banished from the Soviet Union. His good friend, President Masaryk invited him to be a guest of Czechoslovakia, where he stayed for nine months. In November, 1923, he came to this country, and the following year was offered a professorship at the University of Minnesota. After six years there, he was invited to be the first professor and chairman of the Sociology Department at Harvard. In 1930, he became a naturalized American citizen. Since that year he has remained at Harvard.

In 1948, Mr. Eli Lilly and the Lilly Endowment offered to sponsor his studies of "how to make human beings less selfish and more creative." Their generous bequest led to the establishment of the Harvard Research Center in Creative Altruism in 1949, which he is now directing.

During his years in America, many distinctions have been awarded him, including Presidency in the International Institute of Sociology, numerous honorary doctorships, and he has published besides his scientific papers, more than a score of substantial volumes.

WALTER A. LUNDEN was born in Minnesota in 1899. He received his A.M. degree from University of Minnesota in 1929 and his Ph.D. from Harvard in 1934.

He taught at University of Pittsburgh from 1931 to 1941 and came to Iowa State University, where he is now Professor of Sociology, in 1947.

During World War I, he served in the U.S. Air Force and returned to the service in 1943 as a Major in the U.S. Army. From 1943 to 1946, he served as a Prison Officer with the British 21st Army and the 7th and 3rd U.S. Army in England, France and Germany. He was Chief of the Prison Branch, OMGB.

3

Books By Pitirim A. Sorokin

CRIME AND PUNISHMENT (1914). In Russian.
LEO TOLSTOI AS A PHILOSOPHER (1915). In Russian.
ELEMENTS OF SOCIOLOGY (1919). In Russian.
SYSTEM OF SOCIOLOGY (2 vols., 1920-21). In Russian.
GENERAL THEORY OF LAW (1920). In Russian.
TODAY'S RUSSIA (1923). In Russian.
ESSAYS IN SOCIAL POLITICS (1923). In Russian.
LEAVES FROM A RUSSIAN DIARY (1924). Revised ed. (1950).
SOCIOLOGY OF REVOLUTION (1925). German ed. (1928).
SOCIAL MOBILITY (1926). Japanese ed. (in part, 1928). Chinese ed. (1930). Spanish ed. (1954).
CONTEMPORARY SOCIOLOGICAL THEORIES (1928). German ed. (1930). Japanese ed. (in part, 1930). Yugoslav ed. (1932). Chinese ed. (1933). French ed. (1935). Second Chinese ed. (1936). Czechoslovakian ed. (1936). Spanish ed. (1951). Polish ed. (in preparation). Ukrainian ed. (in preparation).
PRINCIPLES OF RURAL-URBAN SOCIOLOGY (1929).
A SOURCE BOOK IN RURAL SOCIOLOGY (3 vols., 1930-31).
TIME-BUDGETS OF HUMAN BEHAVIOR (1939).
SOCIAL AND CULTURAL DYNAMICS (4 vols., 1937-41). Spanish ed. (in preparation). Hindustani ed. (in preparation).
CRISIS OF OUR AGE (1941). Portuguese ed. (1954). Norwegian ed. (1948). Czechoslovakian ed. (1948). Spanish ed. (1948). German ed. (1950). Dutch ed. (1950). Finnish ed. (1952). Japanese ed. (1954).
MAN AND SOCIETY IN CALAMITY (1942).
SOCIOCULTURAL CAUSALITY, SPACE, TIME (1943). Spanish ed. (in preparation).
RUSSIA AND THE UNITED STATES (1944). Portuguese ed. (1946). British ed. (1950). Japanese ed. (1953).
SOCIETY, CULTURE, AND PERSONALITY (1947). German ed. (in preparation). Italian ed. (in preparation). Spanish ed. (1957).
RECONSTRUCTION OF HUMANITY (1948). Japanese ed. (1951). German ed. (1952). Norwegian ed. (1953).
ALTRUISTIC LOVE: A STUDY OF AMERICAN GOOD NEIGHBORS AND CHRISTIAN SAINTS (1950).
SOCIAL PHILOSOPHIES OF AN AGE OF CRISIS (1950). German ed. (1953). Spanish ed. (1954).
EXPLORATIONS IN ALTRUISTIC LOVE AND BEHAVIOR: A SYMPOSIUM (1950). French ed. (in preparation).
S.O.S.: THE MEANING OF OUR CRISIS (1951). Czechoslovakian ed. (in preparation).
ESTRUCTURA MENTAL Y ENERGIAS DEL HOMBRE (1952).
THE WAYS AND POWER OF LOVE (1954).
FORMS AND TECHNIQUES OF ALTRUISTIC AND SPIRITUAL GROWTH: A SYMPOSIUM (1954).
FADS AND FOIBLES IN MODERN SOCIOLOGY (1956). Spanish ed. (1957).
THE AMERICAN SEX REVOLUTION (1956).

Books By Walter A. Lunden

THE DYNAMICS OF HIGHER EDUCATION (1939).
SYSTEMATIC SOURCE BOOK IN JUVENILE DELINQUENCY (1938).
STATISTICS ON CRIME AND CRIMINALS (1942).
BASIC SOCIAL PROBLEMS (1950).
CASES ON SOCIAL LEGISLATION (1950).
OFFENDERS IN COURT AND IN PRISON (1955).
A DEMOGRAPHY OF DELINQUENCY (1956).
THE COURTS AND CRIMINAL JUSTICE IN IOWA (1957).

CONTENTS

PREFACE

Most of the hitherto dominant Sensate Political Institutions, Values, and Ideologies have increasingly become obsolescent and disserviceable. Their creative genius has notably evaporated; their inspiring fire is largely gone, and its ashes are turning cold. There remain now only the empty shells of these previously great Institutions, Values, and Ideologies. By inertia these shells are still crackled and clashed one against another by politicians, ruling *elite,* and their ideologists in their incessant fight with one another. But this fight has also become largely obsolescent and increasingly dangerous for well-being and survival of mankind. For its very survival and for continuation of its creative history mankind is forced to assess soberly the deadly perilous situation it is facing, and to look for the new Political Institutions, Values, and Ideologies that can meet successfully the gigantic challenge of our time. In a very small way this work endeavours to contribute to this assessment and to the quest for the new, better and nobler, Political and Social Order in human universe.

Dedication of the book to President and Mrs. Henry Noble MacCracken of Vassar College is a token of a deep appreciation of their generous help to the senior author at a difficult period of his life, after his arrival in this country, in 1923.

For assistance in compiling some of the data of this work we are indebted to Francis D. Smith; for editorial assistance, to Albert C. d'Amato.

For financial help in the execution of this study, our thanks are due to Eli Lilly and the Lilly Endowment, Inc.

PITIRIM A. SOROKIN, Harvard University
WALTER A. LUNDEN, Iowa State College

INTRODUCTION

The Momentous Questions of Our Time

The well-being and survival of the human race are today largely determined by a mere handful of the top rulers of the great nuclear powers. In the hollows of their hands they hold the monopolistic control of unprecedented deadly weapons. Upon their wisdom or stupidity largely depends mankind's fate — lasting peace or suicidal war. Never before in history has the life or death of so many depended upon so very few! The greatest autocrats of the past had but a fraction of the tremendous power held now by a few members of the Politbureau or the top leaders of the United States ruling *elite*.

This dangerous situation naturally raises the momentous questions of our time: Can we entrust the fateful decision of war or peace — and through that the "life, liberty and pursuit of happiness" of hundreds of millions of human beings — to the few magnates of this power? Do they have the wisdom of the serpent and the innocence of the dove necessary to lead us to a lasting peace and a magnificent future?

For our part we are inclined to answer these questions in the words of the Psalmist: "Put not your trust in princes [and rulers] . . . in whom there is no help" (Psalms, 146:3). This advice, so correct in regard to the rulers of the past, is particularly timely in its application to contemporary governments. The gigantic tasks of peacefully resolving the tremendous difficulties of the present, of preventing new wars, and securing man's creative progress, cannot be entrusted to the existing governments, and especially to "the nuclear governments" of the great powers.

Still mainly tribal governments of politicians, by politicians, and for politicians, today's ruling groups do not display the minimum of intellectual, moral, and social qualifications necessary for a successful solution of these tremendous tasks.

In the first place, throughout history the moral integrity of powerful governments has been — and still is — too low and their criminality too great to entrust to them the life and well-being of mankind. Secondly, a fruitful resolution of these problems far exceeds the creative ability of the existing governments. Thirdly, a constructive realization of human aspirations demands: a) a replacement of these "governments of politicians" by "governments of scientists, saints, and sages"; b) an establishment of certain conditions, such as universal and total disarmament which can automatically prevent misuse and abuse of power by each and every government; c) a substitution of the largely obsolescent political ideologies and current tattered values by new ones, better adapted to meet the gigantic challenge of this new era; and finally, d) the spontaneous mobilization and inspired cooperation of all the creative forces of humanity — its best minds, purest hearts, and highest consciences — for building a nobler and better order in the human universe.

In the light of these reasons, to entrust mankind's destiny and survival to the monopolistic decision of the existing governments is a very poor gamble, even the utmost folly on the part of every member of the human race.

Let us more closely examine these facts and determine to what extent they are factually and logically valid.

CHAPTER I

IDEOLOGIES OF RULING GROUP
MORALITY: THREE VIEWS

Since the moral integrity of governments must be established in order to warrant committing the "life, liberty, and pursuit of happiness" of millions of fellowmen into their trust, our first inquiry is: how good has been the actual moral behavior of rulers in general and of the magnates of power of the existing governments specifically? This pregnant question was raised long ago and since ancient times has received three different answers: 1) unconditionally glorifying; 2) approving from the standpoint of a *double moral standard;* and 3) finding dualistic moral behavior and more criminality than among the ruled populations.

1. IDEOLOGIES GLORIFYING THE RULING ELITE

The central point underlying diverse glorifying ideologies is the claim that the moral standards of rulers and governing elite are far superior to those of the rank and file of the ruled. In past empires — the Egyptian, Babylonic, Summeric, Iranic, Hittite, early Greek, Roman, Byzantine, Mayan, Arabic, Mediaeval European and others — this sort of ideology was based upon belief in the superhuman nature of pharaohs, monarchs, other rulers and governmental leaders. They were deified and worshipped as gods or gods' representatives by religious cults of the respective populations. Their divine powers and virtues were eloquently expressed in their exalted titles, sanctioned by law and moral precepts and justified by various philosophies and ideologies. They were extolled by rich mythologies; glorified by heroic sagas, poems, and epics; immortalized in magnificent pyramids, palaces, temples, castles, and in countless other architectural, sculptural, numismatic monuments and paintings. Their stories have been told in songs, hymns, anthems, prayers, oratorios, and operas; dramatized by splendid ceremonies, rituals, and plays. Initiated and actively spread by the rulers themselves, all known forms of propaganda and techniques of indoctrination have been used to impress indelibly the ruled population with the beliefs in the divine life and mental and moral superiority of the ruling elite.

Since these rulers have been declared gods or gods' representatives, they have naturally been placed beyond the law and above all moral precepts. The Roman legal formulae: *princeps legibus solutus est,* and *quod principi placuit legis habet vigorem* ("the chief is above the law," and "whatever the chief pleases has the power of law") typically express the belief in the superhuman morality of rulers. More familiar sayings — "the king can do no wrong" or "government by the grace of God" — are variations on this same theme. The rulers' superpompous titles in which they declare themselves gods, or the rulers of heaven and earth, omnipotent, omniscient, unfailingly just and as perfect as the gods themselves, epitomize this ideology.

In more modern governments the myth of the moral and mental superiority of their rulers is based less upon religious and more upon so-called metaphysical, mystical, rational, positivistic, utilitarian, and even scientific reasons. These glorifying philosophies and political theories instruct us that the morality of the governing elite is supreme and impeccable because the rulers are "superhuman heroes," mysteriously elected and anointed and because they represent government "of the people, by the people, and for the people." Because the election-process itself somehow confers upon the rulers the grace of moral perfection and is evidence of their moral superiority; or because the rulers are supremely endowed by heredity; or because of destiny, biological and social selection, or good luck, they are blessed with wisdom and virtues; or their high position is a sufficient evidence of their superiority, for otherwise they would not be rulers; and so on. Rulers of state governments and of other powerful groups are still widely believed to be the true moral leaders, protectors of justice, defenders of divine and human law, heroic examples and incorruptible pillars of the supreme moral virtues.

In hundreds of different ways these reasons are developed in modern ideologies which glorify the recent governments of states and of other powerful religious, business, and labor organizations. These ideologies are succinctly expressed by various titles such as "Your Majesty," "Your Highness," "Your Holiness," "Your Eminence," "Your Grace," "Your Honor," "Your Excellency," "Your Splendour," "Your Nobility," and so on, which in countless ways — and according to the official protocol of ranks and precedences — are daily used in all existing societies. The rulers themselves, their official

and unofficial ideologists, and millions of allegedly
scientifically minded citizens still firmly believe in the
rulers' supreme moral integrity.   In predominantly
secular words these ideologies deify, glorify, and exalt
contemporary political bosses, especially dictators.
Lenin and Stalin, Mao-Tse-tung, and Hitler have
been called: "the Savior of Humanity," "the greatest
leader among all the great leaders of the human
race," "the greatest genius" in science and arts,
philosophy and ethics, politics and economics, military strategy and the moral ennoblement of man.   In
all fields of social and cultural creativity, this deification is done not only in daily papers and political
speeches, but in scientific and philosophical publica-
tions.   In any Soviet scientific journal chosen at
random, one can find Lenin or Stalin referred to as
the highest authority in all the natural sciences,
humanities, and social disciplines.   Quotations from
them are used as the ultimate evidence of truth
in exactly the same sense that theologians use quotations from the Sacred Scripture.   The same can be
said of the German deification of Hitler in the Third
Reich, of the Chinese glorification of Mao-Tse-tung
throughout Communist China, and of the cult of
other dictators in the totalitarian governments of our
time.

In a slightly milder form similar exaltations of
Churchill, F. D. Roosevelt, de Gaulle, Adenauer,
and other presidents, prime ministers, generals, mar-
shals, and top officials of democratic countries are
incessantly spoken, not only by themselves and their
retinues, also by millions of "enlightened" citizen-
voters of these nations, by their democratic and so-

cialistic press, radio, television; by their columnists, scientists, philosophers, artists, literati, religious, civic, business and labor leaders. Citizens sincerely call their rulers saviors of our nation, incorruptible defenders of freedom and justice, leaders who successfully solve all the difficult problems of our time, and they believe that to their wise and just decisions the very life and destiny of mankind can be confidently entrusted.

Like the ancient deified autocrats, contemporary political bosses unblushingly immortalize themselves in monuments, statues, paintings, universities, libraries, museums, mausoleums, and other magnificent buildings. Blaring their names, streets, highways, towns, cities, parks, dams, regions convey the message, as do their speeches and articles, memoirs, biographies and such forms of highly paid art as loud advertising and blatant propaganda. Merely listening to the orations at the major political conventions or to the speeches of a major electoral campaign leads one to realize that there is hardly any basic difference between the deification of ancient tyrants and glorification of the top rulers of today's totalitarian and democratic nations. Such has been the answer to our momentous question.

These ideologies represent non-empirical beliefs or emotional dithyrambs of the believers to their idols and are largely outside the realm of provable fact or scientific theory and criticism. Everyone is entitled to believe as he will, to be crazy in any way he pleases, so long as the believer does not enthusiastically coerce these beliefs upon his fellowmen. If, however, the idolators of rulers seriously endeavor to claim scientific validity for their beliefs, their contentions can be easily disproved and decisively declined.

Their unconditional glorification of rulers as either gods or their direct representatives is based on an assumption which is either false or totally unverifiable. None of these points has ever been proved, and most of them can never be proved. The same can be said of modern modifications of these beliefs in the form of the outlined metaphysical, mystical, rational, utilitarian, and pseudo-scientific ideologies of the moral superiority of rulers. None of these theories gives the barest minimum of empirical or logical evidence for valid corroboration of its claims. An important role in historical and social life does not make these beliefs scientific, and they belong to the realm of mythology and emotional fantasy rather than to the field of science.

2. MACHIAVELLIAN IDEOLOGIES: A DOUBLE STANDARD

The ideologies claiming a double standard of morality readily grant that, if judged by the legal and moral standards applied to the populace, or by the imperatives of natural law, the moral behavior of rulers is often unlawful, wicked, and criminal. But, according to these theories, the morality of ruling elites should be judged by a special code of political precepts quite different from the ethical code of the ruled. A special code is dictated by the very nature of governing activities. A successful discharge of their functions and duties requires from the rulers a systematic commitment of actions which, if committed by the ordinary citizens, would be declared immoral and criminal by the enacted laws of their nations. For the vital interests of national security, justice, well-being, prosperity, stable order, and progress, governments are entitled to ignore and transgress all laws and precepts obligatory for the ruled, when reasons of state demand such transgression.

For the same reasons their behavior and policies have to be free from the stricture and control of the common legal and moral codes. There must be and there is a dualism between political action and moral action. Political action cannot be judged as good or bad from the moral standpoint. It is impossible to take part in politics and keep one's hands clean. In the interest of the state one must, if necessary, break a promise or commit murder. Public morality is outside of private morality, and evil, murder, and crimes are permissible to the rulers when they are committed for the good of the state.[1]

In political action everything becomes a "means" to the political end, whether it be morals, religion, or law. Rulers are entitled to carry out any kind of policy necessary for achievement of their political purposes. The very success of the immoral policies is ample justification of their morality, while the failure of the ethical policies is evidence of their political unfitness. The truly great rulers have never hesitated to use criminal means in their successful policies, while the poor rulers have often failed, being the victims of their own moral integrity. As a rule, the amoral and criminal policies of the great rulers have been more beneficial to their people than the moral policies of the poor rulers.

Such are the leading principles of the ideologies of a double moral standard. Like the "divine right" ideologies, they emerged long ago and have been frequently reiterated up to the present time. Their ancient example is given in the Instructions of the Pharaoh Amenemhet (of the Twelfth Dynasty) to his son:

> Hearken to that which I say to thee, that thou mayest be king of the earth, that thou mayest be ruler of the lands ... Harden thyself against all subordinates. The people give heed to him who terrorizes them; approach them not alone. Fill not thy heart with a brother, know not a friend, nor make for thyself intimates ... When thou sleepest, guard for thyself thine own heart, for a man has no people in the day of evil.

Subsequently these and similar precepts have many times been repeated by many a ruler and by a legion of ideologists of double standard morality. "The states are not ruled by prayer books," remarks Cosimo di Medici. The misdeeds of the ruling group are a part of "divine providence," beneficial for the people (Zuccola). "Strong men are the best rulers and from their harsh rule come the civilized and refined societies ... Through acts of violence rulers renew their strength, and out of their misdeeds and criminal acts comes the good society" (G. Vico). *Qui nescit dissimilare nescit regnare* (He who does not know how to dissimilate does not know how to rule), advises Louis XI of France. His counsel is reiterated by Louis XIV's instruction: *N'ayez jamais d'attachement pour personne* (Never have attachment for anyone) and by Napoleon's statement: "If the people say that the king is kind, this means he is a poor ruler." Similar principles have been enunciated by many rulers of Egypt and Babylon, China and India, Iran and Rome, Russia, Europe, and other countries.

These ideologies have been more fully developed by many thinkers of ancient, mediaeval, and modern times, like the "Indian Machiavelli," Kautalya (in his *Arthasastra*), Yang Choo in China, Thrasymachus, Thucydides, Callicles, Carneades, Sextus Empiricus, and Lucian in the ancient Greece and Rome; by Pierre du Bois, Marsilio of Padua, Machiavelli, Vico, Bodin, Hobbes, Croce, Sorel, Pareto, Lenin, Stalin, Hitler, Mussolini, and other defenders of rulers' freedom from moral restrictions, of the autonomy of politics from ethics, of the justification of a morally reprehensible but successful policy by its very success, of subordination of all values to the level of mere means for political ends.

Of all these ideologists, Machiavelli, in his *Prince,* formulates this theory of a double morality in what is possibly the clearest and most pointed manner of all:

A man who wishes to make a profession of goodness in everything must necessarily come to grief among so many who are not good. Therefore it is necessary for a prince, who wishes to maintain himself, to learn how not to be good, and to use this knowledge and not use it, according to the necessity of the case.

I know that every one will admit that it would be highly praiseworthy in a prince to possess all the qualities that are reputed good, but as they cannot all be possessed or observed, human conditions not permitting of it, it is necessary that he must not mind incurring the scandal of those vices, without which it would be difficult to save the state, for if one considers well, it will be found that some things which seem virtues would, if followed, lead to one's ruin, and some others which appear vices result in one's greater security and wellbeing.

From this arises the question whether it is better to be loved more than feared, or feared more than loved. The reply is, that one ought to be both feared and loved, but as it is difficult for the two to go together, it is much safer to be feared than loved, if one of the two has to be wanting. For it may be said of men in general that they are ungrateful, voluble, dissemblers, anxious to avoid danger, and covetous of gain; as long as you benefit them, they are entirely yours; they offer you their blood, their goods, their life, and their children, as I have before said, when the necessity is remote; but when it approaches, they revolt. And the prince who has relied solely on their words, without making other preparations, is ruined . . . Love is held by a chain of obligation which, men being selfish, is broken whenever it serves their purpose; but fear is maintained by a dread of punishment which never fails.

When the prince is with his army and has a large number of soldiers under his control, then it is extremely necessary that he should not mind being thought cruel; for without this reputation he could not keep an army united or disposed to any duty. I conclude, therefore, with regard to being feared and loved, that men love at their own free will, but fear at the will of the prince, and that a wise prince must rely on what is in his power and not on what is in the power of others.

How laudable it is for a prince to keep good faith and live with integrity, and not with astuteness, every one knows. *Still the experience of our times shows those princes to have done great things who have had little regard for good faith, and have been able by astuteness to confuse men's brains, and who have ultimately overcome those who have made loyalty their foundation.*

A prince being thus obliged to know well how to act as a beast must imitate the fox and the lion, for the lion cannot protect himself from traps, and the fox cannot defend himself from wolves. One must therefore be a fox to recognize traps, and a lion to frighten wolves. Those that wish to be only lions do not understand this. Therefore a prudent ruler ought not to keep faith when by so doing it would be against his interest, and when the reasons which made him bind himself no longer exist. If men were all good, this precept would not be a good one; but as they are bad, and would not observe their faith with you, so you are not bound to keep faith with them. Nor have legitimate grounds ever failed a prince who wished to show colourable excuse for the non-fulfilment of his promise. Of this one could furnish an infinite number of modern examples, and show how many times peace has been broken, and how many promises rendered worthless, by the faithlessness of princes, and those that have been best able to imitate the fox have succeeded best. But it is necessary to be able to disguise this character well, and to be a great feigner and dissembler; and men are so simple and so ready to obey present necessities, that one who deceives will always find those who allow themselves to be deceived.

A certain prince of the present time, whom it is well not to name, never does anything but preach peace and good faith, but he is really a great enemy to both, and either of them, had he observed them, would have lost him state or reputation on many occasions.

Hatred is gained as much by good works as by evil, and therefore, as I said before, a prince who wishes to maintain the state is often forced to do evil, for when that party, whether populace, soldiery, or nobles, whichever it be that you consider necessary to you for keeping your position, is corrupt, you must follow its humour and satisfy it, and in that case good works will be inimical to you.[2]

Such is the answer of the double morality ideologies to our question.

The nature of this answer at once raises a question, as to whether the very principle of a double morality is itself admissible and valid? If the principle serves a *cognitive* purpose in the sense of giving to us a correct factual knowledge about the moral behavior of the ruling groups (compared with that of the ruled), then it has a *scientific* value and justification for its admissibility. Likewise, if the principle of a double ethical standard serves *an ethical* purpose of either *moral and legal ennoblement* of the rulers and the ruled or gives a valid *moral and legal basis* for justification of violations of moral imperatives and law obligations by the rulers, then it has *moral and legal reasons* for its admissibility. If it does not serve these — scientific or ethical — tasks, it undermines all ethical values and leads to demoralization of the rulers and the ruled.

Instead of increasing our empirical knowledge about the moral behavior of the rulers, the principle of double morality only blears and confuses it. A careful reading of the above excerpts from Machiavelli's *Prince* and of other quotations shows them as neither scientific statements about the actual moral behavior of the rulers nor as supreme moral and legal formulas for the conduct of the rulers; the ideologists of double morality themselves state that truly virtuous conduct of the rulers shall comply with the moral and legal imperatives promulgated by the supreme moral commandments and laws of their society. In Machiavelli's terms, the truly virtuous rulers "should be all mercy, faith, integrity, humanity, and religion." It is absurd to insist that their transgressions become virtues and their wicked and their unlawful actions moral and lawful conduct. This is an indication of the ambiguity of the ideologies of double morality: self-contradictory propositions which are neither factual description of the real behavior of rulers nor moral and legal precepts.

There are still other reasons for rejection of this double moral standard. First, when developed consistently, this line of thought leads naturally to the familiar precept: "rulers can do no wrong." It puts the rulers over and above law and all moral values. It leads to a complete absolution of the rulers from all morally horrible and legally criminal actions. Through that, it erases the very boundary line between the right and wrong, the criminal and the lawful, the good and the evil. It ends in a complete moral nihilism. Instead of answering our question about the comparative morality or criminality of the rulers and the ruled, such a nihilism annihilates all moral distinctions, and, with it, throws out of the field of investigation the question itself.

Second, the double moral standard leads to the same result in another way: if we accept this absolution of the rulers from all their sins and crimes, no comparative study of the criminality of the rulers and the ruled becomes possible; since the rulers cannot be criminal, there remains only the criminality of the ruled.

Third, by introducing different measuring sticks these ideologies make the measurement itself impossible; for whatever commensurable is being compared and measured, the measuring stick or unit must be the same.

Fourth, the principle of a double moral standard means an extreme relativization of moral precepts and legal imperatives. It makes the same precept or law-norm, for instance, "Thou shalt not kill" obligatory for some (in our case, for the ruled) and non-obligatory for others (for the rulers). In this way an unlimited atomization of moral and law-values is introduced. Their imperatives are made contingent on and relative to whom they are applied. Elsewhere[3] it is shown that when not only the secondary, but the *basic* moral values are declared to be relative, such a step unavoidably leads to a universal progressive atomization of these values until they are ground into dust and become devoid of any binding or motivating power.

This atomization of moral values and imperatives engenders conflict. This, in turn, produces hatred, which leads to rude force and bloodshed. In the chaos of conflicting and arbitrary moral norms, might inevitably becomes right, and the result is *bellum omnium contra omnes* ("War of everyone against everyone"). The inevitable collapse of the whole fabric of moral and legal values ensues and leads again to a total nihilism and legal anarchy.

Fifth, the basic moral commandments and the basic law-imperatives are enacted as norms of moral and legal conduct binding upon all members of a given society, the rulers and the ruled. The Ten Commandments, the Sermon on the Mount, the Bhagavad-Gita, the basic moral precepts of Taoism, Confucianism, Hinduism, Buddhism, Jainism, Judaism, Mohammedanism and of any true ethical system are addressed to all. They do not make any exception or reservation for rulers.

Such a standpoint of the actual moral codes of conduct does not give any factual ground for the moral irresponsibility of the rulers.

In this point we agree with the position of Lord Acton, that "the Ethics of History cannot be denominational." In his correspondence with Creighton, he states that he cannot apply a double moral standard to kings and other rulers "with a favorable presumption that they did no wrong." Criticizing Creighton's double moral standard he continues: "You would hang a man of no position, like Ravaillac (the assassin of Henry IV, of France); but if what one hears is true, Elizabeth asked the gaoler to murder Mary, and William III ordered his Scots minister to extirpate a clan. Here are the greater names coupled with the greater crimes. You would spare these criminals, for some mysterious reason. I would hang them, higher than Haman, for reasons of quite obvious justice; still more, still higher, for the sake of historical science."[4] ·

No more convincing is the ideologists' argument about the motives and reasons such as: "reasons of state," "the wellbeing of the people," "the salvation and security of the nation," which allegedly justify criminal actions of ruling elite and make them non-criminal or lawful. Indeed, most of the legal codes mention a number of cases of this sort and explicitly absolve rulers from the criminality of certain well specified actions committed for some reason of state or in the public interest. But the number of such exceptions is limited and most of the gravest crimes are not excused in this manner. Practically all legal codes[5] hold rulers morally and legally responsible for such criminal actions. None of these codes entitles the rulers to commit murder. The same is true in regard to treason and other grave crimes against person, the state, property, religion, and so on. Since these codes hold them responsible, the apologists of the double moral standard do not have any factual ground for their "superindulgent attitude" toward the criminality of rulers.

Moreover, in most of the cases it remains questionable which motivations the rulers really have in committing this or that criminal act. Like most human beings, rulers tend to rationalize, beautify, and justify all of their criminal deeds by claiming allegedly non-selfish reasons for their commitment: *salus populi suprema lex, raison d'etat,* the good of the nation, in the public interests, and so on. Factually, in almost all such cases their personal — and ordinarily selfish — reasons play the dominant role, while the unselfish motives are mostly an eye-wash staged to gratify the rulers themselves and to mislead the ruled.

Even when an unselfish motive really is responsible for the ruler's crime, there is question as to whether such a motive can turn a criminal action into a non-criminal one. It is possible that the prevention of civil war or other reasons of state and of public interest were the main motives in ordering the "legalized" murder of their sons by Peter the Great of Russia and by Abbas the Great of Persia; or in the "legalized" murder of his wives by Henry VIII; or in the personal killing of his son by John the Terrible; or in Stephen Dushan's strangling of his father; or in Empress Irene's blinding her son; or in Empress Theophano's assassination of her husband; or in Sviatopolk's murdering his two brothers; or in the purging of their friends and murdering thousands of innocent persons by Cromwell, Robespierre, Lenin, Trotsky, Stalin, and Hitler, and in hundreds of similar murders by rulers. Does such a motive justify these actions morally? Can it make them non-criminal legally? Finally, can this sort of conduct serve as a universal moral example to be imitated by everyone?

The negative answer to all these questions is self-evident. The hypothetically assumed unselfish motive in no way justifies these actions morally, nor does it make them non-criminal legally; nor does it depict these rulers as the social heroes worthy of universal imitation. What these actions reveal is the utter moral savagery of these rulers and their complete inability to control their basest impulses. If this sort of moral conduct of the rulers is imitated by the ruled and by everybody, then a total — moral, mental, and social — anarchy is bound to explode within a short time.

This sort of argument of the criticized ideologists is but a variation of the familiar motto: "The end justifies the means." We know well that in almost all actions and policies of this sort the evil means usually become the real end and the good end fades and remains forgotten.

No more convincing is the claim that the institution of government itself and its inevitable misdeeds are the lesser evil in comparison with the graver ones inherent in the human race and pervading all society. We are told that for this reason the misdeeds of the rulers are not only excusable but they are real virtues beneficial to mankind and to each of the ruled nations. The ancient — Biblical and other — myths about the Fall of the initially innocent man exemplify this sort of ideology.

> When mortals were bent on doing their duty alone and habitually veracious, there existed neither [government], nor lawsuits, nor hatred, nor selfishness. The practice of duty having died among mankind, lawsuits have been introduced; and the king has been appointed to decide lawsuits, because he has authority to punish.

> In former ages men were strictly virtuous and devoid of mischievous propensities. Now that avarice and malice have taken possession of them, [governments] and judicial procedures have been established.[6]

> After the Fall and the establishment of government "for the king's sake the Lord created Punishment, the protector of all creatures, an incarnation of law. . Through fear of it all created creatures . . . swerve not from their duty. . Punishment alone governs all created beings. . Without it the

stronger would roast the weaker, the crow would eat the sacrificial cake. . ownership would not remain with anyone, the lower ones would usurp the place of the higher ones. The whole world is kept in order by punishment, for a guiltless man is hard to find. . All men would rage against one another in consequence of mistakes with respect to punishment. But where Punishment with its red eyes stalks about, destroying sinners, there the subjects are not disturbed, provided that he who inflicts it discerns well."[7]

The central idea of these ancient ideologies is sound: the society of perfect and innocent men scarcely needs any coercive government with compulsory laws and merciless punishment. It is also true that in a society of vicious and beastly men any government under laws that are not too unjust is a lesser evil than no government and no law at all; even a poor law-order is better than an unlimited lawlessness; even a limited coercion of government is preferable to the beastly war of everyone against everybody.

However, these considerations do not justify the evil actions of rulers, nor do they justify the existence of governments which engender and promote their societies' demoralization; nor do they cause such actions and governments to become virtuous and praiseworthy. The ancient myths of the Fall and the precepts for rulers' conduct are more sound than the yarns of the ideologists of the double morality: the ancient myths and beliefs emphatically condemn the violations of their duties by rulers and never forget to stress: "provided that the ruler who inflicts punishment discerns well" (The Laws of Manu);

that "the king is holy in acts and speech, fully instructed, pure, of subdued senses, impartial towards his subjects;"[8] that "the king does not flourish unless he has virtues,"[9] that "the king who does not do his duty becomes liable to perform penance," and that violations are to be punished in this and in the other world.[10]

Similar warnings are found in Chinese, Egyptian, Judaistic, and other ancient moral and legal instructions for rulers.

The totality of the above considerations is sufficient to show the scientific as well as the ethical invalidity of the Machiavellian ideologies of double morality.

3. Critical Ideologies: Least Rule is Best

The third type of theory regarding the morality of rulers and the institution of government is critical and condemnatory. This attitude also emerged in the remote past and has been reiterated up to the present time. Taoism gives a classical example of this kind of interpretation and evaluation of government-institution and of morality of rulers. In its essentials, Taoism is a philosophy of Being vs. Becoming. It stresses the eternal all pervading, permanent Tao vs. the everchanging appearances; inaction vs. being in perpetual motion and agitation; control and minimization of desires vs. their maximalization and unbridled satisfaction; uselessness, even harmfulness of energetic governments vs. glorification of strong rulers and reformers. The following quotations from the text of Taoism illustrate these points.

There was something, undifferentiated and yet perfect, before heaven and earth came into being. So still, so incorporeal! It alone abides and changes not. It pervades all. It may be regarded as the mother of all things. I know not its name: if I must designate it I call it Tao. Man takes its norm from earth; earth from heaven; heaven from Tao; the Tao from itself.[11]

The mind of man loves stillness, but his desires draw it away. . When no desire any longer arises, there is the true stillness and rest. In constant stillness there is the constant purity and rest.[12]

I consider doing nothing to obtain enjoyment to be great enjoyment [or "doing nothing better than to be busy doing nothing"]. Heaven does nothing, and thence comes its serenity. Earth does nothing, and thence comes its rest. All things in all their variety grow from this inaction.[13]

The wise man will have no desires or ambitions, no aims, no purposeful and energetic activities: then everything will go right of itself.

The more restrictions and prohibitions are in the empire, the poorer grow the people. The more weapons the people have, the more troubled is the state. The more there is cunning and skill, the more startling events will happen. The more mandates and laws are enacted, the more there will be thieves and robbers. Therefore the holy man says: I practice nonassertion, and the people of themselves reform. I love quietude, and the people of themselves become righteous. I use no diplomacy, and the people of themselves become rich. I have no desire, and the people of themselves remain simple.[14]

In a perfect consistency with these principles Taoism formulated the most radical *laissez faire* attitude in

regard to government and its activities. Some of
the Taoist formulas in this matter (e.g. "The best
government is that which governs the least," or "a
social reformer is the most impractical of men,")
have been repeated again and again in subsequent
centuries by such thinkers as Thoreau and Leo
Tolstoy. It is an axiom for the Taoists that a ruler
or king does not differ from a brigand, and that both
are foolish and wicked.[15]

Critics such as Godwin, Spencer, Gumplowitz,
and Oppenheimer contend that the state itself and
any state government were created mainly by war
and other aggressive activities. For this reason the
states and governments cannot help being centralized
power mechanisms or systems of organized violence,
indifferent to moral requirements, and preoccupied
mainly with power-politics. Other critics stress
the fraud, lies, hypocrisy, economic exploitation,
merciless brutality, lust for domination, greediness,
and other ethically reprehensible characteristics of
builders and rulers of empires. The central ideas of
these ideologies are typically illustrated by the following excerpts:

The militant type [of society] is one in which the
army is the nation mobilized while the nation is
the quiescent army, and which, therefore, acquires
a structure common to army and nation. . The
centralized control, necessitated during war, char-
acterizes the government during peace... The
absoluteness of a commander-in-chief [who usually
becomes the head of the government in such so-
cieties] goes along with absolute control by his
generals over their subordinates: all are slaves to
those above and despots to those below. . [Religion

also becomes a militant religion of enmity]. [Industry and labor of the subordinated population] exist solely to supply the needs of the governmental-military structures.. Not industry only, but life at large is subject to [detailed and rigid] discipline [and regimentation].... The liberty and the claims of the individual are nothing.. Absolute subjection to authority is the supreme virtue and resistance to it is a crime.. The will of the citizen in all transactions, private and public, is overruled by that of the government. The cooperation by which the life of the militant society is maintained, is a *compulsory* cooperation.[16]

Thus the rulers of militant, totalitarian, socialist or welfare types of states turn "the life, liberty, and pursuit of happiness" of their subjects to their own ends. They ascribe to themselves the absolute power of doing whatever they wish to do with their slave-like subjects.. While the governments of Europe divide the regions of the backward peoples among themselves with cynical indifference to their needs and demands, there is no reason to expect that these governments would pay any attention to the interests of their own citizens. So-called Christian governments continue to glorify military brigandage as the highest virtue and great conquerors like Alexander the Great, Charlemagne, Peter the Great, Frederic the Great, and Napoleon as the greatest heroes of the human race.[17]

In each country and in each region some feudal lord, more cunning, and often less scrupulous, had succeeded in appropriating to himself richer personal domain, more peasants on his land, more knights in his following, more treasures in his chest... The germ of a future state was thus laid.

This state and its lord eventually enslaved free population, and replaced its free mutual aid by coercion and exploitation.[18]

However power [of government] has been gained, those who possess it are in no way ... more disposed than others to subordinate their own interests to those of society. On the contrary, having the power to do so at their disposal, they are more disposed than others to subordinate the public interests to their own. On the other hand, the true Christian doctrine, making of the law of love a rule without exceptions ... abolished the possibility of any violence, and cannot help but condemn every state founded on violence... [19]

Leave us alone. If you, emperors, generals, judges, bishops, professors, if you have need of armies, navies, courts, prisons, gallows, guillotines, prepare them all yourselves; tax yourselves, judge yourselves, imprison and execute yourselves, get yourselves killed in war; but leave us alone, for we have no need of all these things and we do not wish to participate in the acts that are so futile and above all, so wicked.

If there is a devil in history, it is this power principle [concentrated in the state and its government]. Together with the stupidity and ignorance of the masses, upon which it is ever based, it is this principle alone that has produced all the misfortunes, all the crimes and the most shameful facts of history. [For this reason the state and its rulers are evil and must be destroyed, if need be, by even violent means] (M. Bakunin).[20]

Power tends to corrupt and absolute power corrupts absolutely ... Great [political] men are almost always bad men ... If the people knew what sort of men statesmen were, they would rise and hang the whole lot of them.[21]

Such, in essentials, is the third answer to our momentous question. Like the preceding two ideologies, the condemnatory ideologies are largely speculative, and do not give sufficiently solid, factual evidence for demonstration of their validity.

In the next chapter we will try to give an answer, which we hope is based on a more systematic usage of the relevant empirical facts than most of the outlined ideologies.

CHAPTER II

MORALITY AND
MENTALITY OF RULERS

The results of our empirical study of moral behavior and mentality of rulers and governments may be summed up in five generalizations. None of these pretends to be an exact, universal, or perennial formula applicable to every ruler or to all chiefs of governments. Every student of history knows well that there have been, and are, good and bad rulers, constructive and destructive governments. Our generalizations are but descriptions of five characteristics or uniformities typical of rulers taken as a group or stratum and compared with that of the ruled populations. In this chapter, for the sake of economy and continuity of our argument, only a few of the proofs are mentioned and only a bare minimum of the explanatory comments is given. The body of empirical evidence from which the generalizations are derived is given in the references found in this book.

1. FIVE GENERALIZATIONS

1. *When the morality and mentality of rulers and the ruled are measured by the same moral and mental yardstick* (and not by the double standard discussed above), *then the rulers' morality and minds appear to be marked by a much stronger dualism— by greater mental and moral schizophrenia than the morality and mentality of the members of the ruled populations.*

2. *The ruling groups contain a larger propor-tion of the extreme mental types of the gifted and the mentally-sick than the rank and file of the ruled populations.* Taken as a whole the ruling groups are more talented intellectually and more deranged mentally than the ruled populations. Furthermore, the ruling strata have a larger proportion of domi-nating, aggressive, highly selfish, bold and adven-turous persons, men harsh and insensitive to other human beings, hypocrites and liars, and cynical ma-nipulators of human relationships, than the strata of the ruled populations.

3. *The moral behavior of ruling groups tends to be more criminal and sub-moral than that of the ruled strata of the same society.*

4. *The greater, more absolute, and coercive the power of rulers, political leaders, and big executives of business, labor and other organizations, and the less freely this power is approved by the ruled popu-lation, the more corrupt and criminal such ruling groups and executives tend to be.*

5. *With a progressive limitation of their power, criminality of rulers and executives tends to decrease qualitatively (by becoming less grave and mur-derous) and quantitatively (by decreasing the rate of criminal actions).* If and when the power of rul-ing bodies is greatly limited (legally and factually) and when the governments function amidst a strongly integrated and unified moral public opinion, their criminality may become equal to or even fall below the criminality of their ruled populations.

2. Factors Responsible for These Characteristics

The nature of the ruling occupation and social selection are probably the main factors of these typical traits of ruling elite. This can be deduced from a careful analysis of the forms of social selection of rulers and the kind of activities contained in the business of ruling, including the focal social position of the magnates of power and the environment in which governing activities are carried on. This means that the five typical features of ruling groups are not so much an expression of rulers' personal wishes and fancies, but that these wishes, fancies, and characteristics are molded and impressed into their mentality and behavior by their occupational activities and by the kind of social selection of rulers prevailing in their societies or nations. Of course, the factors of biological heredity and marginal free choice also play some role, but this role finds its actual manifestation exactly through the mechanism of social selection and through their occupational functions. Therefore, these additional factors are taken into consideration and included among the factors responsible for the characteristics discussed. Let us now briefly comment on them.

3. Moral Dualism of Ruling Activities

Viewed from a moral standpoint, ruling functions consist of two profoundly different, even strikingly opposite, activities; some tend to morally ennoble rulers while others stimulate their demoralization and criminality.

Ennobling Activities of Rulers. There is no doubt that the occupational functions of rulers contain several morally ennobling activities such as: the protection of life, security, freedom and other rights of the citizens; defense of the country from foreign enemies and of innocents from the attacks of aggressors; the discharge of justice and maintenance of law and order; the prevention and suppression of crimes; educational and social service work; the amelioration of economic and cultural conditions of the people; the stimulation of creativity and preservation of vital, moral, and mental well-being of the population; and the legion of other constructive, charitable and socially beneficial functions performed by executive, legislative, and judicial branches of governments. These and similar activities tend, almost automatically, to develop the rulers' moral integrity, sense of justice and social responsibility, compassion, benevolence, and unselfishness. One who daily performs this sort of activity for months and years can hardly escape some retroactive ennobling influence. For this reason, there almost always are, even in heartless and wicked rulers, a few important moral virtues habitually acquired in the process of their ennobling occupational work.

Long and regular discharge of these altruistic functions develops in the majority of rulers some notable virtues and, now and then, a moral nobility of the highest kind. However, for reasons indicated in the next paragraph, these virtues rarely permeate the whole personality of rulers and rarely manifest themselves in all their activities. As a rule, this moral excellence is confined within a limited portion of rulers' mentality and behavior, beyond which they may remain immoral, even criminal. Nevertheless, within this ennobled part the "soul" of rulers is indeed pure and sometimes even "holy", and their overt actions represent a true fulfillment of the noblest moral imperatives.

Criminalizing and Demoralizing Activities of Rulers. The discussed moralizing activities of rulers cover only a part of their total occupational functions. The other part of these activities exerts upon the rulers morally deadening and criminalizing effects rather than uplifting and ennobling ones. Let us consider some of these criminalizing activities:

1. A considerable part of the criminalizing functions of rulers is represented by their violent, destructive, and murderous activities — activities which characterize much of the total behavior of governments. War activity can serve as an example of this kind of occupational function; the planning, preparing for, and carrying on of war has always been practically the main preoccupation of rulers. Stripped of its propaganda, war activity is the most terrible form of organized mass-murder, supplemented with other acts of human bestiality, lust, and sadistic-masochistic destructiveness. No war activity can be carried on without throwing to the wind, at least temporarily, all the moral imperatives. No man preoccupied with war activities for years and years, can escape the demoralizing and criminalizing effects of this murderous business.

Other murderous activities of rulers deaden their moral sensitivity, and harden their souls and hearts towards the lives and values of human beings.

Directly and retroactively these activities contribute
to demoralization and criminalization of rulers. The
activities of condemning and executing "criminals",
exterminating dangerous "revolutionaries" and "sub-
versives", eliminating possible competitors; suppres-
sing disorders, riots and revolts; punishing the violators of law; sacrificing many an "expendable"
human life in training for and performance of government functions by military, police, and other
agencies of the government — these serve as examples of violent and destructive actions. Practically no government of an empire or of other powerful organizations can help becoming a mass ex-
ecutioner and "legalized" murderer. Such an activity is inherent in and inseparable from the business
of ruling vast organizations. And all the branches
of government participate in this murderous activity
— the legislative when it enacts the laws imposing
capital and other punishments for violation of its
statutes; a judge when he imposes the death sentence
or other severe punishment upon the "guilty criminal;" an executive agent (beginning with monarch,
president, general, admiral, and ending with a private, policeman, or warden) when he enforces the
enacted laws and court-sentences; and all the
branches together when they declare a war or other
bloody reprisals against their collective enemies,
criminals or opponents. This murderous activity
comprises a large part of the business of practically
all rulers of powerful, coercive organizations.

2. Another governing activity consists of what
is called "diplomatic" actions and operations. These
activities are sometimes performed for the protection

and expansion of selfish interests of the government
and sometimes for the tribal interests of the governed group; sometimes to reconcile conflicting interests and mitigate clashes of various factions and
persons or for the realization of other mainly egotistic purposes. Diplomatic operations exhibit a
peculiar mixture of honest and dishonest techniques
of influence by means of organized spying, skillful
lies, hypocritical assurances, false promises, threats
and bribes, semi-rational persuasions, limited coercion, cloak and dagger actions, cynical machinations,
and other morally doubtful procedures.

By their very nature, the "murderous" and
"diplomatic" activities of government are sub-moral
and potentially criminal. Committed by a private
person, they would be condemned as unlawful and
therefore punishable.

3. The third "criminalizing ingredient" of
governing consists in the incessant bombardment of
government by a multitude of contradictory interests
of various persons and groups. The government is
the focal point of the relentless pressures of clashing
interests which the rulers, as legislators, judges, or
executives, have incessantly to resolve. These pressures generate inner conflicts in the minds and conduct of the rulers. When one is subjected continuously to the contradictory stimuli of this sort, one's
moral integrity and mental sanity tend to become
fragmented, confused, and often self-contradictory.
Pushed and pulled in opposite directions by these
pressures, one's judgement and actions are bound to
be more or less inconsistent and unsound, and one's
personality increasingly neurotic.

In addition to this, many influential and rich parties reinforce their pressure by bribery of the rulers, offering economic and other advantages, by flattering and catering to their lusts, appetites, ambitions, and fancies; and even threatening them with retaliation (death, overthrow, etc.) if the rulers fail to decide the clash of interests in their favor. When one is continuously subjected to this kind of pressure, one is liable to succumb to some temptations and eventually allow his conduct to become determined mainly by unethical and unlawful motivations. In theses two ways, this ingredient leads the rulers to moral and mental aberrations.

4. The fourth "criminalizing component" of governing activity is the enormous power which the rulers of vast organizations hold over millions of the ruled population. It is said that power intoxicates and a great coercive power intoxicates doubly. These observations were formulated long ago and, as we have seen in the preceding chapter, have been since reiterated by shrewd observers of human affairs and eminent social thinkers. In recent times similar propositions have been set forth by many a scholar and thinker. F. Dostoievski's statement admirably sums up these conclusions:

When a man has unlimited power over the flesh and blood of his fellow men, when a man is in a position to degrade another human being to the limit of degradation, he is unable to resist the temptation to do wrong. Tyranny is a habit. In the end it becomes a disease. The best man in the world becomes so brutalized as to be undistinguishable from a wild beast. Blood intoxicates, the spirit becomes susceptible to the extreme

abnormalities and these can turn to be enjoyable
as the real joys. The possibility of such license
sometimes becomes contagious in a whole people;
and yet society which despises the official hangman, does not despise the hangman who is all
powerful.[1]

Thus power intoxication marks a large portion
of the top rulers of the political empires in Ancient
Egypt and Babylon, in Ancient Rome and Greece,
Iran and India, China and Japan, Europe, the
Americas, and of practically all the states and powerful political organizations. Before achieving supreme power many of these rulers (especially the
revolutionary leaders) were normal; later, many of
them became abnormal human beasts. Rulers' power
generates in them (and in others, too), a belief that
they are the chosen and anointed who are far above
the ruled population and its common-herd moral and
legal precepts of right and wrong, good and evil.
Indeed, most of the powerful monarchs, dictators,
"protectors of people," presidents of republics, senators, generals, and other political bosses believe
themselves to be a superhuman or superior elite
whose wishes and decisions create law. In brief,
they see themselves as essentially free from the limi-
tations of unpleasant legal obligations and moral imperatives. Such a freedom amounts to a moral and
legal nihilism. In this way "power tends to corrupt"
and "absolute power corrupts absolutely."

These four components of governing activity
generate and develop criminal and unethical tendencies in the rulers of powerful organizations. Systematic and continuous use of the outlined pro-

cedures by the members of ruling groups turn these practices into habits which eventually become part and parcel of their personalities and behavior. Living in this atmosphere of murderous and "diplomatic" activities, and practicing them daily, subjected to incessant temptations and intoxicated with power, the ruling group cannot escape the inevitable contaminating and demoralizing effects. For comprehensible reasons, in their declarations the rulers naturally assert their unlimited devotion to the supreme and sacred value of individuals, but in their overt actions they rarely practice the precepts of their eloquently preached sermonets. They tend to regard their subjects as a mere number — cannon fodder, voting herd, or expendable material — for manipulation and realization of their tasks.

Such are some of the factors of amorality and criminality inherent in the governing activity of monarchs, presidents, dictators and bosses of powerful social organizations.

5. *These factors, inherent in the business of ruling, are reinforced by factors of social selection.* Not all types of individuals have an equally strong desire to become ruler; nor do all of the types have an equal chance to succeed in this ambition. Some are persons dominated by a lust for power, while others have no such ambition. Other conditions being equal, the non-ambitious type of person is bound to be less frequent among the rulers than the power-hungry type. Furthermore, individuals with high moral sensitivity, compassion, honesty, and altruism have much less chance to climb to the high rungs of the government ladder than those who are

callous, unsympathetic, aggressively selfish, hypocritical, dishonest, and cynical manipulators of human
relations.

Stern ruling or money making; conquest or dictatorial domination; building political or economic
empires; spreading religion or revolution by bombs
and murder; discharging acts of merciless justice;
maintaining social order by cruel punitive measures;
pitiless elimination by dishonest means of competitors for high political or economic position — these
and other ruling functions demand for their successful performance the proverbial tiger's ferocity, rhi-
noceros' insensitivity, and fox's wiliness in handling
their subjects and fellowmen. A perfectly sincere
man can hardly become a successful diplomat, or a
compassionate humanitarian a terrible conqueror;
an honest person who makes no hyperbolic promises
has little chance to be elected for a high political
position; a businessman who unfailingly follows the
Golden Rule can hardly build an economic empire
in a cut-throat competitive business world. Insin-
cerity, insensitivity, and a cynical manipulation of
convictions and values seem to be necessary pre-
requisites for successful social climbing.

4. Rulers and Their Symbols

The heraldic symbols with which rulers identify
themselves on their coats of arms, in their titles or
nicknames admirably express these characteristics.
Lion, tiger, eagle, cobra, vulture, wolf, crocodile, fox,
hawk, dragon, and other carnivorous, predatory,
poisonous, or wily creatures are the most frequent
symbols of rulers' self-identification. No less reveal-

ing are their "historical nicknames" chosen by the rulers themselves instead of their real names, like: Stalin (the Man of Steel) in lieu of his real name: Djugashvili; Molotov (the Hammer) instead of Scriabin; Kamenev (the Stone) in place of Rosenfeld; or such historical "thumbnail" characteristics as: Genghis-Khan "the Mighty Killer," Attila "the Terror of the World," Tamerlane "the Scourge of God," Ivan "the Terrible," Yamashita "the Tiger of Malaya," Clemenceau "the Tiger," Antonescu "the Red Dog," and then a long row of "Earth-Shakers," "Conquerors of the World," "Kings of Kings," "Rulers of the Universe," "Iron" Emperors, Dukes, Chancellors, and so on, and so forth. The prevalent mechanisms of political selection decidedly favor social climbing into the ruling strata by this sort of person. One would look in vain among great political rulers, captains of industry, mighty conquerors, or eminent revolutionary leaders for a "soft," sentimental, humane, timid, sincere, and entirely honest individual. At best, only very few may be found. Genghis-Khan or Napoleon, Attila or Tamerlane, Cyrus the Great or Thutmosis III, Peter the Great or Mohammed, Marius or Sulla, Torquemada or Pope Gregory VII, Charles V or Caesar, Cardinal Richelieu or Zishka, Carnegie or the founders of the Rothschilds, Lenin or Hitler, Stalin or Mao-Tzetung, Oliver Cromwell or Robespierre, Louis XIV or Charlemagne, Catherine the Great or Elizabeth I, Frederick the Great or Henry VIII, W. Churchill or Bismark, the Sparton aristocracy or the Roman patricians, the Venetian aristocracy or the Spanish conquistadors, the first Merovingians or the Carolingians; the founders of the medieval noble families or that of the Vanderbilt, the Rockefeller, and the Astor Empires — these and thousands of other "builders" are well symbolized by the discussed heraldic coats of arms and nicknames. Many of them, for the success of their business, have sacrificed their own parents or children, murdered their closest friends, and ruined their benefactors. Other leaders, who do not exhibit conspicuously the savagery of a lion, display in its place the cynical cunning of a fox or craftiness of a cobra. They are especially numerous among politicians and money makers of so-called democracies. Aristides, Mazarin, Metternich, Talleyrand, Lloyd George, Disraeli, Briand, and many leaders of the recent political parties are the examples of crafty machinators of values, human beings, and social relations. They have an extraordinary talent for proving today that A is B and tomorrow that A is non-B, and always in the name of God, humanity, liberty, justice, progress, and other slogans. It does not matter here whether these machinations are good or bad. What matters is that they are demanded by the nature of the business of the ruling classes.

5. Personality Traits and Power Rule

Only when a given ruling elite begins to decay do these traits tend to disappear. In their decaying stage the ruling strata become uncreative, timid, and soft. But as soon as this happens, they tend to be overthrown and superseded by bold, harsh and wily newcomers. The same may be said of the aristocracy of wealth.

"The Brahmin aristocracy has been severe, and it has existed for at least 2,000 years. The Spartan aristocracy was stern and cruel, and it ruled during at least seven centuries. As long as the Venetian aristocracy was severe and wily, it successfully kept its power. The early medieval nobility and the Normans were severe. And, in spite of many great revolts, they successfully kept their domination. On the other hand, as soon as an aristocracy became humanitarian and afraid to use violence, it usually was overthrown. Such is the situation in all prerevolutionary periods. Aristocracy and the kings of the prerevolutionary periods are invariably soft, impotent, mild, liberal, humanitarian, and effeminated. As a result, they are put down."[2]

Studied from a psychiatric standpoint, social selection appears to favor three types of individuals attaining public office: (1) the inadequate psychopath, placid and emotionally blunt, often mistaken for a profound person; (2) the aggressive, obsessive-compulsive boss, conceited, ambitious, domineering, and intolerant; (3) the ethically aberrant personality, often endowed with an acute intelligence but morally wily and cynical.[3]

To sum up: the outlined (1) murderous and (2) "diplomatic" activities of rulers, (3) their position as the focal point of various contradictory and often corruptive pressures, (4) the power of rulers, and (5) the prevalent mechanisms of social selection are the main criminalizing factors of ruling groups. These demoralizing forces are inherent in the ruling of empires and vast organizations as they have been governed up to the present time.

6. The Moral and Mental Dualism of Rulers

The preceding discussion shows that the business of ruling consists largely of two opposing kinds of activities in curious relation to each other. The ruler's noble actions in one area usually occur side-by-side with debasing criminal actions in another. Often these two conflicting elements are fused, as in the case of a ruler employing ignoble means to achieve humanitarian goals, or using noble actions as a facade to mask his baser intentions. These contradictory activities generate conflict in the character of the ruler which, when reinforced by the factors of social selection, creates a split in his personality, making him a sort of Dr. Jekyll-Mr. Hyde. This basic dualism manifests itself in most rulers, making them appear at some times generous, altruistic, and morally noble, and at others selfish, criminal, and inhuman; their behavior seems to alternate between intelligence and folly, health and neuroticism. This does not occur in the same proportion among all governments and rulers. In some ruling groups the criminal tendencies prevail, while in others the morally ennobling properties are dominant. Despite this diversity, a moral and mental schizophrenia seems to characterize all forms of government which govern mainly by murderous, "diplomatic" and other compulsory means.

These conclusions seem to be verified by striking contrasts between the behavior of a ruler in his ruling capacity and his behavior in private life. Robespierre, as dictator of the Jacobin government in France, showed himself to be a blood-thirsty and merciless tyrant who sent hundreds of victims to the guillotine without compunction. Yet, in his private life, this same man proved to be so tender-hearted that he would weep over the sentimental novels of B. de Saint-Pierre! Lenin, acting as a ruler, unhesitatingly ordered the shooting of thousands of innocent persons, yet in the privacy of his apartment, was deeply concerned over the health of a slightly sick kitten. Similar split personality was shown by Stalin, Hitler, Napoleon, Peter the Great, Cromwell, Charles V and Phillip II of Spain, Louis XIV, Henry VIII, Elizabeth I, Nero, Diocletian, Constantine the Great, Asoka, and by most monarchs, dictators, commanders, inquisitors, etc. In a milder form, this moral schizophrenia also marks the high ranks of democratic government personnel: political and military leaders, top executives of big corporations, labor leaders, and even the hierarchy of vast religious and scientific organizations.

In regard to the business executives the dualism is once more confirmed by the recent study of 162 American business executives by E. E. Jennings and associates of Michigan State University's Business Administration College. The study shows that "the typical executive is apt to lead a double life with one set of principles for the office, another for home and church. . A Jekyll-and-Hyde strain runs through their ranks. . Ambitious business executives do not regard as success-contributing those practices ordinarily regarded as good human relations. . They believed that self-interest was the basis of all human nature, that it was safer to be suspicious of men and assume their nature was more bad than good."

The executives avoided making close friends in areas crucial to their interests, regarded past promises not binding if they stood in the way of success, kept secret advantageous information, and so on; in brief, in their office they followed Machiavellian ethics while at home they practiced the principles of good citizenship. (The Boston Daily Globe, April 10, 1959, A.P.)

This dualism is also demonstrated by the strikingly high percentage of extreme mental and moral types among the rulers. P. Jacoby, F. A. Woods, P. A. Sorokin, and other investigators of the mental and moral properties of monarchs unanimously agree that *the percentages of geniuses as well as of the feebleminded and insane is much greater among the royal families than among the general population.* Also, the frequency distribution among monarchs in the categories of: above average, average, and below average differs quite markedly from the frequency distribution of scholastic grades among the students of our colleges.

Documentation. Of the 354 monarchs studied by F. A. Woods, 143 were above average, 135 were below average, and only 76 belonged to the average group. Of the 352 monarchs studied by Sorokin, 15 per cent fell into the superior class, 8.5 per cent were failures (feeble-minded, insane, demoralized, or incapable),[4] the remaining 76.5 per cent made up the average class. Although in this study the percentages of the extremes (superior and failures) are lower than in F. Woods' study, they are far greater than the somewhat similar percentages of feebleminded and insane among the general population, as well as the percentage of "A" students in our colleges. In 1910 the percentage of those hospitalized for feeble-mindedness or insanity in the United States was only about 0.8 per cent in the cities and 0.4 per cent in the country. In 1920, among the recruits ranging in age from 18 to 30, only 1.15 per cent were diagnosed as being mentally deficient, neurotic, or psychotic. At the other extreme, only about 5 per cent of the students in our colleges can be classified as "A" students. Although the percentages of the mentally gifted and mentally defective fluctuate greatly from country to country and from period to period, the percentages of these extremes remain notably lower among the general population or a college population than among the rulers. Significantly Sorokin's study "shows a correlation between the per cent of "A" and "Failures" among the monarchs: the higher the first, the higher the second. The examples of Russia and Turkey are especially conspicuous in this respect." Whereas the per cent of "A" monarchs for the whole group of 352 monarchs is 15 and the per cent of "Failures" is 8.5, corresponding percentages for the Russian monarchs are 16 and 12, and for the Turkish sultans 20 and 20.[5]

This prevalence of extremes among the rulers is at least partly due to the dualistic or schizophrenic nature of the governing activity (and partly to hereditary factors). Other studies have shown that the contradictory situations in daily governing activities tend either to develop inner conflicts and split personality within rulers, or to polarize them into the extreme mental, moral, and social types, or to turn

them into confused, hesitating, and self-contradictory individuals whose right hand denies what their
left affirms.[6]

Reading or listening to the important addresses of
monarchs, presidents, and high dignitaries of states
or other powerful organizations, one notices glaring
contradictions within the same speech or declaration.
For instance, many of them proudly declare themselves and their policies to be Christian, often quot-
ing the Sermon on The Mount and other precepts of
Jesus as the guide to their policies. A few minutes
or lines later, without hesitation, they proclaim in
effect: therefore, in the name of Jesus, let us crush
and exterminate our enemies; let us reduce their
cities and countryside to ashes; let our nuclear and
bacteriological weapons teach them an unforgettable
lesson, and so on. In the first chapters of the same
work some of them (like Lenin) pompously declare
that their purpose is the elimination of the state and
coercive government, and in subsequent chapters
they conclude: therefore, we must establish the iron
dictatorship of the totalitarian regime in which the
Communist government regiments the whole life,
conduct, and thought of the ruled population.

In recent decades, practically all governments
and the United Nations have repeatedly declared
that their main task is the establishment of a lasting
peace. Yet at the same moment, these rulers by
their acts refute this goal for they limitlessly arm
themselves, carry on cold wars, and thus prepare to
exterminate hundreds of millions, at the risk of an
Apocalyptic war which can terminate the very existence of life on this planet. Such speeches can be

heard or read daily. Although their contradictory topics and precepts may vary, they display the peculiar "illogical logic" symptomatic of the split and sick soul.

This schizophrenic dualism can easily be seen in a comparison of the main principles of the rulers' addresses with their overt actions of implementation. Almost invariably an unbridgeable chasm is found to exist between these preachings and their practices. Any sincere believer in God, or in the values of Truth, Justice, Beauty, Peace, Equality, Progress of Mankind, Wellbeing of Humanity, Democracy, Freedom, Brotherhood, Socialism, Communism, and so on, cannot help but deplore the utter distortion of these values in the practices of the rulers who preach them. Viewed dispassionately, many of the actions of crusaders of God are more sacrilegious and atheistic than those of the avowed atheists and anti-religionists. Many an action of the ruling propagandists of the Dictatorship of Proletariat, Democracy, Freedom, Brotherhood, etc., are anti-proletarian, anti-democratic, tyrannical and anti-brotherly.

These and other proofs confirm our diagnosis of the mental and moral dualism of governing activities and its effect upon the personality and conduct of rulers and governments.

CHAPTER III

CRIMINALITY AND MORALITY OF HEADS OF STATE

The outlined moral and mental duality of ruling operations and governments does not necessarily mean that both the benign and the evil characteristics are equally powerful in every ruling individual, or that they are distributed in the same proportion among all governments and rulers. There are ruling groups in which criminal tendencies prevail, and there are governments in which the benign nature is dominant. Whether one of the two souls is generally prevalent among all the rulers and governments remains largely unknown and needs to be studied further. A further inquiry is needed also to obtain a more accurate knowledge of what kind of ruler (and in what socio-cultural conditions) tends to be predominantly sunny-souled or dark-souled. Finally, the moral dualism of rulers and ruling activities tells little about the comparative criminality of the rulers and the ruled: which of these classes is the more criminal? The purpose of this chapter is to give a tentative answer to the last question and thereby to elucidate a little the other two.

The generalizations: Nos. 3, 4, 5, formulated at the beginning of the preceding chapter, give tentative answers to these questions. In their essentials these answers contend that when measured by the same stick, the moral behavior of ruling groups tends to be more criminal than that of the ruled population in the same society; and that with a progressive limitation of the power of rulers and executives their criminality tends to decrease in frequency as well as in gravity of crimes committed. This analysis of criminalizing factors of rulers and bosses of vast organizations gives deductive reasons for these generalizations, derived from the analysis of the nature of the ruling occupation and from the prevalent forms of social selection. Now these deductive conclusions must be tested and confirmed empirically through a study of the factual criminality of the ruling and the ruled strata. It is the task of this chapter and the one following to examine the facts about rulers, titular and actual, as well as other power elements in the modern state.

1. CRIMINALITY OF MONARCHS

Of all big social organizations the state, as a rule, is the most cynical and most naked power-machinery. With rare exception, this machine of organized coercion is more powerful than that of almost any other organization. The sovereignty claimed by the state as its monopoly is the official term designating its supremacy over other social groups. The chiefs of states, especially when they are autocratic or absolutistic, are the most powerful rulers among the governing heads of other social bodies.

If our generalizations (Nos. 3, 4, 5) regarding the criminality and morality of rulers are correct, they should be confirmed by the actual conduct of the state rulers. This expectation is well supported by the relevant facts.

First of all, despite the lack of precise and systematic statistics, the existing data do not allow any doubt that the *powerful and/or autocratic rulers of the states display in general a much higher rate of patricides, matricides, fratricides, uxoricides, and murders of their relatives, than does their ruled population.* In regard to this crime, the powerful autocratic ruling groups are possibly the most criminal groups in the total population of most nations or states. We must keep in mind that this particular form of murder is evaluated by practically all criminal codes as the gravest form of murder and is uniformly punished more severely than all other forms (except the murder of the rulers of the states and other power organizations). Second, the existing body of evidence shows also that *with a limitation of the autocratic or absolute power of the rulers, the gravity and the rate of their criminality tends to decline.* Murder and other bloody crimes against relatives, friends, and persons generally tend to be increasingly supplanted by the crimes against property, and by the lesser crimes against person. Criminality of these rulers whose power is greatly limited (like most of the recent constitutional monarchs and presidents of republics) tends to approach the criminality of their ruled population, though it still exceeds it.

Actually the criminality of the rulers remains much greater than the percentages show, when we compare the percentages of all kinds of murder (and not only the murder of relatives and friends hitherto discussed) committed by the rulers, with those of all kinds of murder perpetrated by the common population. Side by side with legal execution of crim-

inals and war enemies, very few of these rulers did
not murder or condemn to death, directly or indirectly, few or many innocent persons of all ages and
of both sexes. Sometimes they imposed the death
penalty over the victims legally, for "reasons of state"
(raison d'etat), though even in such "legal" murders
there always is a wide gulf between the merciful and
sadistic interpretation of "legality." More frequently
the rulers condemned to death many an innocent
person for such selfish reasons as economic advantages, hedonistic pleasure, revenge, hatred, sadistic
drive, sexual motives, lust for power, rulers' security,
and so on. Perhaps still more frequently they
"eliminated" innocent persons because these individuals by their mere existence happened to inhibit
the realization of the rulers' egotistic objectives. This
sort of motive plays an eminent part in the mass-
murders of hundreds and thousands of innocent persons in the massacres, "crusades," "purges," "liquida-
tions," "holy wars," "restorations of order" always
solemnly declared "for the Good of the Country,"
"Nationalism," "Purity of Race," and all sorts of
justifying catchwords and mottoes aimed at screen-
ing the ugly selfish interests of the rulers. These
mass-murders of thousands of innocent persons depict the heartlessness, moral insensitivity, and cynical
disregard of human life and moral values which
characterize the rulers. In this regard, their psychology is not very different from that of hardened murderers. Such "murders" are so common that they
are often passed over by historians without mention,
yet study reveals that the ruling group is indeed the
most murderous group among all the groups of the
ruled populations of almost all countries or nations.

An additional oblique confirmation of this conclusion is given by the exceptionally high frequency
of *death by violence* among state-rulers. Being little
inhibited in their struggles for power from murdering relatives, friends, competitors, and anyone who
happens to be hindering satisfaction of their objectives, these rulers are treated to similar "murderous"
treatment by their competitors. The ruling group
well confirms the truth of the old statement: "He
who takes the sword shall perish by the sword."

Finally, regarding the crimes of aggravated assault, rape, and other sex offences, robbery, burglary,
theft, larceny, embezzlement, fraud and forgery, and
other lesser crimes against person, property, and
good mores, the rates of the rulers in these crimes are
again much higher than those of the ruled.

Ordinarily, when the rulers perpetrate crimes
against property, they do not steal, or grab or rob or
forge or embezzle a few dollars or a small piece of
real estate, or a few precious objects. Instead *they
do these crimes on the largest scale,* grabbing by "the
right of conquest" vast regions, territories, and kingdoms; under false pretense expropriating and appropriating large fortunes and sources of wealth of their
adversaries or citizens; by "diplomatic" persuasion
and coercion acquiring big estates, fabulous monopolies and most profitable privileges; profiting greatly
by debasing the currency, and so on. An old English
poem well expresses this large scale of the crimes of
rulers:

"The law locks up both man and woman
  who steals the goose from off the common,

but lets the greater felon loose,
who steals the common from the goose."

To sum up: in the crimes enumerated the criminality of the rulers is many times higher than that of the total ruled population.

2. HISTORICAL DOCUMENTATION

For our first evidence of the criminality of rulers, we may compare them to the ruled population in the crime of murder. Since there are only fragmentary data about the rates of murder of relatives for the total or adult (fourteen years old and over) populations, we shall compare the rulers' murder of their relatives with those of all kinds of murder for the total populations (murder of relatives makes up only an insignificant fraction of the larger class of murder generally). Both of these rates are approximate but, despite this, they disclose the difference in criminality to be so great that it remains striking even when the rates of the rulers' criminality are decreased ten or twenty or more times.

Depending upon the period, country, occupation, sex, age, race, etc., the murder rates for the ruled population fluctuate between: 0.0008 and 0.2 per 100 persons of the total or the adult population or of the main occupational populations, or far below one per cent for the ruled populations. For the murderers of relatives among rulers the following gives approximate data:

Of 43 English monarchs and the Lord-Protectors beginning with William I and ending with

George VI, some twenty rulers, or at least *40 per cent,* were guilty of this crime. In other words, the rate of English rulers committing the gravest form of murder is more than a hundred times greater than the rate of the British population in the crime of murder!

This conclusion must be supplemented by the fact that, with the legal and factual limitation of the power of English monarchs, they have freed themselves from this crime; none of the kings or queens since William III has been guilty of murdering his or her relatives or close friends and associates.

Similar data for the rates of murder of relatives and close friends for monarchs and rulers of various countries and periods naturally vary greatly, but they invariably remain far above the rates of general murder among their subjects. With various upstart rulers, of past and recent times, such as the Ten and the Thirty Tyrants in Ancient Greece, Marius and Sulla, Caesar and Anthony, Crassus and Augustus in Rome, Cromwell and Robespierre, Mussolini and Hitler, Lenin and Stalin, and many of today's dictators or revolutionaries in Europe, Asia, Latin America, and elsewhere, the crime-record is still worse than that of the legitimate, autocratic monarchs.

Of the 34 Turkish sultans, from Osman (1290-1326) up to Mahomet VI (1918-1922), at least 14 sultans or some *41 per cent* were guilty of direct or indirect murders of their relatives, close friends, and associates. But here again, with a partly factual and partly legal limitation of their power, the last five sultans, beginning with Abdul Mejid (1839-1861) and ending with Mahomet VI (1918-1922) seem to have been free from this form of murder (with a possible exception of Abdul Hamid II).

Similarly, in France, in the earliest Merovingian dynasty, its founder Clovis (481-511), his four sons, including the victorious Lothair (558-561), and Lothair's four sons, up to Lothair II and his son Dagobert (628-638) were all fratricides or the murderers of their close relatives in their intra-family struggle for power. Not very different was the situation in its declining period when the Merovingian dynasty divided into several branches. All in all, no less than 40 per cent of the Merovingian rulers committed the discussed gravest form of murder.

Perhaps somewhat lower was the per cent of this sort of murderer in the subsequent dynasties of the Carolingians, the Capets, the Valois, the Bourbons, the Orleans, the Bonapartists. Of some 51 rulers, beginning with Charles the Bald (843-877) and ending with Louis Napoleon III (1852-1870), at least 9 rulers or 15 per cent were guilty of this gravest of murders. Except perhaps for Napoleon I, none of the post-revolutionary monarchs whose power was greatly limited, seems to have committed this crime.

Similar is the record of the Russian rulers. As usual, the earliest Kievan (Rurik) dynasty begins its dominion by murders of the related and unrelated competitors for power: Oleg killed Askold and Dir (882). Then came the dynastic warfare between the sons of Sviatoslav, ending with the victory of Vladimir the Saint (972-978), and followed again by merciless dynastic struggle among the sons of Vladimir in which his eldest son, Svyatopolk, murdered his three brothers (Boris, Gleb, and Sviatoslav). Svyatopolk perished in his turn after being defeated by his brother, Iaroslav the Wise (1019-1054). The fratricidal war was again repeated among the sons of Iaroslav, then among the sons of Vladimir Monomakh, and the subsequent generations of the branches of the Kievan dynasty up to the invasion and subjugation of Russia by the Mongols after the battle of Kalka (1223) and during two centuries of Tartar domination.

All in all the per cent of the murderers of relatives, friends, and associates among the Kievan (Rurik) dynasty with its branched Volyn, Galicia, Susdal, Vladimir, and Novgorod rulers was *above rather than below some 25-30 per cent.*

Among subsequent rulers of Russia, one notable difference in the Moscovy period was the vogue of blinding and physical mutilation of "the dear but dangerous relatives" (with subsequent banishment, imprisonment or monastic isolation for life), or the infliction of slow death instead of a direct and swift murder Prince Vasiliy the Dark ordered blinded his Cousin, Vaciliy the Squint-eyed (c. 1435); Prince Dimitri blinded his cousin (c. 1437), and so on. Otherwise, Yuriy Danilovich and Michail Tversky both perished in their warfare with each other; so also did Alexander Tversky and Ivan Danilovitch and other rulers of this period. Later on, the Czars of Muscovy and Russia killed their sons and cousins, (like John the Terrible and Peter the Great), gave consent to the murder of their parents (like Alexander I), or of their wives or husbands or relatives (like Catherine the Great, Elizabeth I) and in various ways executed their close friends and counsellors; this is not to mention imprisonment, torture, banishment, and other methods of "purging" of all those whom for some or no reason at all they wanted to eliminate. All in all, at least some 20 to 25 per cent of the rulers of Muscovy and then of Imperial Russia were guilty in the crime discussed. On the other hand, after Alexander I (1801-1825), all subsequent Czars of Russia up to the last Czar, Nicolas II, were free from this crime.

Similar also is the record of other ruling groups of the past. Thus out of 51 rulers of Ancient Rome from 135 B.C. to 285 A.D. (beginning with T. and G. Gracchus and ending with Probus and Carus) 26 or some 50 per cent were guilty of the crime discussed.

In Byzantium, "no sovereign was safe. Of the 107 sovereigns that occupied the throne between 395 and 1453, only 34 died in their beds, and 8 in war or by accident. The rest either abdicated — willingly or unwillingly — or died violent deaths by poison, smothering, strangulation, stabbing, or mutilation. In the space of these 1058 years we can count 65 revolutions, in palaces, streets, or barracks." "The Sacred Palace of Byzantium is full of grim stories. There the devout Irene had her son Constantine VI blinded in the very room he was born. There in 820, in St. Stephen's chapel, Leo V, the Armenian, was assassinated. . There Basil the Macedonian and his friends slew Michael III; and there also, one December night, Theophano had her husband, Nichephorus assassinated and displayed from a window to soldiers of the guard the severed, dripping head of their master."[1]   Hardly less than 50 per cent of the Byzantine rulers were murderers of their relatives, close friends, and associates.

No better is the record of the Arabian dynasties. A fratricidal struggle for power started immediately after the death of the founder of Mohammedanism, and all four of "the Orthodox Caliphs" (632-661) were guilty of the crime discussed. If all the rulers of the subsequent dynasties of the Umayhads (661-750) and of the Abbasids (750-1100), before and after the dismemberment of the Caliphate into several dynasties were not guilty, then at least some 45-50 per cent committed it in various forms.

If from the Arabian rulers we turn to those of Iran or Persia, we find out of nine kings of the earliest Achaemenian dynasty of Persia (550-330 B.C.) from Cyrus the Great to Darius III Codomannus, at least 3 or some 30 per cent were involved or guilty of the crime. Of some 21 shahs of the Neo-Persian Empire of the Sassanians (226-651) at least seven rulers (or some 34 per cent) murdered their relatives, close friends, and associates. Of some 11 shahs of the Safavid dynasty (1500-1736), at least four or some 36 per cent were guilty of this crime. Other short-lived dynasties of Persia show still higher incidence.

Direct and indirect murder of relatives, closest friends and associates as frequently marks the annals of the Oriental dynasties as the others. Thus, for example, in Japan, at an early period of Japan's history, the chronicle mentions that the rulers of the Soga clan crushed their rivals (c. 587); that Soga

Imago (c. 626) murdered his nephew, the Emperor
Sushun; that in 643 Soga Iruka forced Prince Yama-
shiro no Oe, heir to the powerful prince Shotoku,
to commit suicide. In their turn the chiefs of the
Soga were overthrown and suffered penalties. The
next Nara period (710-784) is marked again by several "family" murders (of Fujiwara Nakamaro,
emperor Junnin, and others); fratricidal civil wars
stamp also the Fujiwara and subsequent periods with
the accompanying murders of relatives and friends
(by Sumitomo, Taira Masakado, Minamoto Yori-
yoshi, Shirakawa II, Taira Kiyomori, Yoritomo,
Hojo Tokimasa and other rulers of the Hojo period,
and by the warring parties during several subsequent
fratricidal wars of the emperors, shoguns and other
rulers). Perhaps it is typical that out of some 15
shoguns of the Tokugawa period (1603-1867), at
least four or some 26 per cent were guilty of murder
of their relatives, close friends and associates. All in
all, some 25 to 30 per cent of the rulers of Japan
seem to have committed this crime.

Out of twelve Inca kings, (from Manco Capac
to Huascar), at least nine, or 75 per cent, are guilty
of these crimes.

If in a similar way we study the rates of crimes
committed by rulers of other states or empires —
China, India, Babylon, Ancient Egypt, and so on
— the main results would be similar to the rough
percentages given. The percentages for different
dynasties and periods may widely fluctuate, but all
would be many times greater than the percentages
of all sorts of homicide for the respective ruled populations. As mentioned, this conclusion remains valid

even if we decrease the above percentage of the rulers' criminality ten, twenty, or fifty times.

The following mass-murders serve as examples of the rulers' massacres of thousands of innocent persons. From 15,000 to 25,000 persons killed in St. Bartholomew Night, in Paris; some 8,000 to 10,000 persons exterminated by the order of Sulla during just one meeting of the Roman Senate;[2] tens of thousands of persons arrested and shot by the order of Lenin after the attempt on his life (the persons who not only did not participate in the attempt, but even did not know anything about it, as Lenin and his associates were well aware). In hundreds of thousands of executions during the years of the Red Terror, they explicitly stated: "Don't look in the records for any crime committed by the executed individuals; they are executed just because they happen to be the members of the bourgeois, or of the kulak-peasant or other potentially anti-Communist classes.") A slaughter of 27,000 captives ordered by Richard the Lionhearted after taking Acca was because the captives could not pay the ransom of 200,000 gold pieces demanded by Richard and the Crusaders (this massacre by "Christian Crusaders" stands in a glaring contrast to the generosity of the sultan Salah-al-Din, the Crusaders' main adversary, who in a similar situation spared the lives of and freed about 20,000 Christian captives). These examples give a fair idea of the mass-murders of thousands of innocent persons by rulers.

In brief, when all sorts of murders by the state-rulers are considered, the per cent of the murderers among them becomes still much higher than that

shown by the percentages of the murderers of relatives and friends. Viewed from this standpoint, *the
ruling group is indeed the most criminally-murderous
group among the populations of almost all countries
or nations.*

The fact of an exceptionally high *death by
violence* among the state-rulers is testified to by the
chart below. The per cent of death by violence
among the rulers of big empires will be shown highest among all the groups of historical persons in
almost all countries and periods.[3]

Categories of Monarchs	Total Number Studied	Number who Died by Violence	Percentage
Roman Empire (including 16 of "provincial" Emperors)	92	61	66.3
Eastern Roman Empire	63	22	34.9
Holy Roman Empire, Austria and Prussia	52	11	21.1
France	77	15	19.5
Russia	26	7	26.9
Turkey	36	9	25.0
England	40	9	22.5
Spain	12	0x	0.0x
Denmark	16	0x	0.0x
Italy (Savoy, Sardinia, Italy)	9	1.x	11.1x
Total	423	135	31.9

x—The absence of the killed here is partially
due to the fact that the kings of these countries are
taken only for the last few centuries (when, as mentioned above, the murderous criminality of the
rulers has tended to decrease in almost all countries
parallel with the limitation of their power and
rights.)

For the purposes of comparison here are the percentages of death by violence among historical persons in the following specified occupations:

Presidents of the			
United States and France	33	4	12.1
Military men	94	19	20.0
Statesmen and politicians	90	9	10.0
Poets, journalists, authors	150	3	2.0
Artists, painters, musicians,			
architects	182	2	1.1
Scientists, scholars	291	1	0.3
Theologians, clericals	130	1	0.8
Lawyers, judges, jurists	49	—	—
Roman Catholic Popes	258	23	9.0
Same after 314 A.D.			
(legalization			
of Christianity)	226	7	3.1*

* The popes before 314 were the victims of persecution by the Rulers of the Roman Empire.

The table shows, first, that 31.9 per cent of deaths by violence among the rulers greatly exceeds the similar percentages among all the specified groups of historical persons. Second, the data show that the next three high percentages (20.0, 12.1, 10.0) are among the military and political leaders, and the presidents of two republics, that is, among the high strata of the rulers, also. Third, that even the popes, so far as they are not only the spiritual, but also the secular rulers, give the fourth highest percentage of death by violence.

Regarding the lesser—but still serious—crimes against person and property, the rulers still remain the most guilty of all.

For the purposes of comparison we can take the

rates for the total population or for the population of 2,640 cities in the U.S.A. for the years 1946 and 1956. If anything, these crime-rates are higher than the rates of those other countries for these crimes. Per 100 population of the United States the rates in the specified crimes are as follows in the years:

	1946	1956[4]
rape	0.008	0.014[4]
other sex offences	0.04	0.087
aggravated assault	0.04	
light assault	0.15	
robbery	0.02	0.060
burglary	0.06	0.449
larceny	0.14	1.228
forgery and counterfeiting	0.008	
embezzlement and fraud	0.014	
stolen property	0.008	

The involvements of rulers in these crimes fluctuate widely from country to country and from period to period, yet in all these fluctuations they remain many times higher than the above rates of the ruled or total populations. Very roughly estimated the percentages of the rulers guilty in committing the crimes *against property are between some 10 to 35 per cent; against persons (except murder and manslaughter) between 20 and 50 per cent; sex offences between 15 and 60 per cent; against good mores, between 10 and 55 per cent.* If we decrease these percentages ten, twenty, or fifty times, they still will be far greater than those for the total populations and one has to keep in mind that only a small fraction of these crimes of the rulers

become publicly known; when committed by the
rank and file, these actions become "crimes"; when
committed by the rulers, they are overlooked or often
are regarded as non-criminal, even virtuous, actions.
Thus a greater part of the rulers' criminality remains
hidden and unassessed.

3. CRIMINALITY OF RULERS OF DEMOCRACIES AND REPUBLICS

Many a reader of the preceding pages undoubtedly has been asking the question: But how about
the constitutional monarchs, presidents, and members of Cabinets, in democracies and republics?
About the leaders of Parliament or Congress? The
supreme judges, the generals and admirals of the
democratic military forces? Governors of democratic
states or provinces? Mayors of the big cities and
other government leaders and political bosses in
democracies? Do the above conclusions apply to
them also? Is their rate of criminality higher, too,
than that of the ordinary citizens or of the total ruled
population? Does not the fact of these rulers being
elected make them paragons of virtue and moral
leaders rather than a criminal group in comparison
with the rank and file population of the democracies?

The general answer to these questions is that
the above conclusions apply also to the ruling
groups in democracies. All in all, their rate of criminality tends also to be notably higher than that of
the total ruled populations.

The main qualification to these statements consists in recalling our second uniformity — that with

limitation of the rulers' power, their criminality tends to decrease in gravity as well as frequency of crimes committed. We have seen that even in limited monarchies their criminality declines, especially in such grave crimes as murder and aggravated assault. Democratic governments are, by law and in fact, greatly limited in their power. For this reason only, their criminality is to be expected to be notably lower than that of the autocratic, powerful governments.

For the same reason, criminality of democratic ruling groups consists mainly in the crimes against property, sex, good mores, and in lighter crimes against person. As a result of this qualitative and quantitative decrease of criminality of the ruling groups in democracies, the contrast between the rates of criminality of the rulers and the ruled (total population) in democracies becomes less great than the contrast in big autocratic empires and nations. Then, under a system of centralized, autocratic power structure the offences tend to cluster about the highest seats of power in each central government. In democratic and limited power structures, without a centralized type of government, criminality tends to diffuse among several strata of governments and among the powerful economic and political groups, formally outside government, which factually are the informal and unofficial partners of the official government and are often more influential than the official ruling groups. Now for a brief corroboration of these conclusions.

1. That the grave criminality of constitutionally (and factually) limited governments —monarchial

or republican — tends to decline is shown by the fact that, after the limitation of their powers, the constitutional rulers of practically all such countries have become almost entirely free from the commitment of murder, aggravated assault and similar grave crimes against person. This can be said of the governments of Switzerland, Denmark, Sweden, Norway, Holland, Belgium, Great Britain, Austria, Germany (up to Hitler), the United States, France, Italy, Russia (up to the Communist Government, 1918, which is by law and by fact, a dictatorial autocracy), Japan, India, and of the constitutional rulers of a few other nations.

2. Despite this moral improvement of ruling groups limited in power, their total criminality still remains above that of the ruled population. This can be deduced easily from a simple confrontation of the rates of criminality of the total populations, with the relevant fragmentary data concerning the criminality of the members of the ruling groups in democracies.

We have seen that the rates of murder for the total populations fluctuate roughly between 0.0008 to 0.2 per 100 persons; while the rates for other crimes are roughly between 0.008 to 1.2 per 100 persons of the total population. Of these rates the maximal rate for murder (0.2) and that for larceny (1.2) are abnormally high, exceptional, non-typical rates. This means roughly that we have in the total populations one murderer per some 500 to 125,000 individuals (500 again being the non-typical exceptional figure); and one criminal in each of the other crimes per some 12,500 to 84 individuals (this latter

in larceny, for 1956, for 80,986,991 urban population of the United States). More specifically, in
the United States, in 1956, there was about one murderer per 20,000 and about one manslaughterer per
28,571 urban population.

Though with a decrease in murder-criminality
of the constitutionally and factually limited governments the democratic governmental groups may not
necessarily be more criminal than the common population, such groups are still as criminal (in these
crimes) and possibly even more criminal than the
total (ruled) population. The United States gives
an example of this situation. As mentioned, in 1956,
in our urban population there was about one murderer per 20,000 and one manslaughterer per 28,571
urban population. Now, in order to have 20,000 and
28,571 high governmental persons in the United
States we shall take: all the presidents and vice-presidents of the United States and members of their
Cabinets; then many (past and present) influential
leaders of the Congress; many top generals and admirals; to these we have to add: a number of (past
and present) governors of the state; mayors and
political bosses of the biggest cities. If we compare
20,000 and 28,571 government personnel of this sort
with the same numbers of non-government persons,
we find somewhat more murderers and manslaugh-
terers within the ruling population. For example,
we find among the twenty leading political bosses
in this country, from 1850 to 1925, at least two who
were indicted for murder (Martin Lomasey and
Richard Crocker).[5] Then, since the mutual killings
of gangsters in their wars are considered murders,

we have to view similarly the killings of each other by members of the different government factions struggling for existence, domination, and spoils. In this category we note the murders of Hamilton, Lincoln, Garfield, H. Long, and others, and the almost fatal beatings (like that of Massachusetts Senator Sumner by Col. Brooks) by adversaries from different "government gangs."

To victims of the civil war between these gangs, we must add thousands murdered in the violent struggle of pro-slavery and anti-slavery factions (like the victims of the violence at Lawrence, in the John Brown revolt, by the Ku-Klux Clan and the Union League) and in other political "wars" between opposite government factions; many an unnecessary murder committed by generals Sherman and Sheridan, governor Stanton, and their adversaries in the Civil War; the murders of large numbers of Indians, without any guilt on their part, with full approval of government agents. Finally, count all the victims murdered by ordinary gang-murderers acting under the order of many political bosses closely connected with, and now and then controlling, the murderous and other activities of the criminal gangs.

When all these and similar murders, committed directly or indirectly by high, middle, and low government agents are counted, the rate of murderous criminality of the total body of government agents is likely to become higher than that of the ordinary ruled population.

Even if the comparative criminal rates depend upon which of the killing actions of government agents are to be considered murder, there is no doubt that the rates of the ruling groups are higher than those of the total (ruled) population, in regard to crimes against property, sex offences, propriety, and the lesser crimes against person. If for comparison purposes we take the above percentage rates of the specified criminality of the urban population of the United States, then we have one sex-criminal (for all kinds of sex offences, including rape) per about 2085 urban population. Now among the presidents of the United States, at least two were guilty of sex irregularities (which would give one sex-offender per some 17 presidential population). If we take a larger stratum of the high government officials (like Alexander Hamilton, and other governmental leaders among the members of the Cabinet, leading members of the Congress, influential governors of the states and top military ranks), their rate in sex-offences appears to be notably greater than the rate for the total or urban population.

Still more certain is the higher criminality of ruling groups in democracies in the crimes against property. According to the above rates in all kinds of crime against property for the urban population of the United States in 1956, we have one criminal per about 370 population. Now, among the presidents of the United States, at least, two were accused of involvement in crimes against property (called often "corruption" and "graft"), perpetrated by their close associates and appointees (this would give one property-criminal per about 17 presidential population). Otherwise, the Cabinet and personnel of the White House staff of practically every administration have produced one or several corrupted officials. In some administrations, like Grant's or Harding's, the corruption exploded into sensational scandals and prison sentences for the offenders.

Crimes of the government officials against property appeared quite early in our history. The first royal governor of the Virginia Colony, Samuel Argall (d.1626) was indicted for corruption in office. These corrupted practices were followed by a great many other governors and rulers of colonial America (Governor B. Fletcher of New York, Samuel Chase, one of the signers of the Declaration of Independence, and a member of the U. S. Supreme Court (1741-1811); Robert Morris (1734-1806), the senator and the financier of the Revolution, and others); and then by the officials of the United States — Federal, State, and Municipal — government. During Jefferson's presidency, 16 out of 29 senators and 29 out of 64 members of the House were unlawful speculators and security holders. A large number of the high-officials, like T. Pickering (1745-1829), general, Postmaster General, Secretary of War and State; House Speaker Dayton (1798-1800); DeWitt Clinton (1769-1828), senator, mayor and governor of New York; Lewis Cass (1782-1866), senator, governor, Secretary of War and Minister to France; William T. Barry (1785-1835), senator and Postmaster General; Stephen A. Douglas — Lincoln's great opponent; Secretary of War Simon Cameron (1799-1889); in Grant's Cabinet, the Secretaries, G. M. Robeson, W. W. Belnap; Congressman Oakes Ames, Vice-President Colfax; William M. Tweed, "Boss Tweed;" Mayor of New York A. Oakey Hall; Secretary of Commerce and Labor

George Cortelyou (1862-1940); Secretary A. B.
Fall, and other members of the Harding Cabinet in-
volved in the Teapot Dome scandal; Mayors of New
York J. J. Walker and W. O'Dwyer (who was also
U. S. Ambassador to Mexico); Mayor of Boston,
Governor of Massachusetts and Congressman James
Curley; "the Bosses," Thomas Pendergast, Mayor
Frank Hague; Tammany Hall bosses Ch. F. Murphy
and G. W. Olvany; in recent times Senators J. M.
Butler, Newberry, F. L. Smith, Hiram Bingham,
Wm. S. Vare, T. G. Bilbo, A. B. Chandler; Con-
gressmen J. M. Coffee, E. Cox, Andrew J. May, J.
Parnell Thomas, W. E. Brehm, Orville E. Hodge;
the mink coat and refrigerator cases in the Truman
White House staff; the Sherman Adams-Goldfine
incident; the misdeeds in the Internal Revenue
Bureau, in the Reconstruction Finance Corporation,
in the Veteran Administration, and other cases in the
Eisenhower administration — these are just a few
typical examples of hundreds and thousands of
property crimes or "improprieties" perpetrated by
the members of the high and middle ranks of the
Federal, the State, and the City governments. These
offences have become so frequent, routine, and expected, that they received even the special terms
of "indispensable and licensed delinquency" and
"honest graft."[6]

To put the matter in different form, we can say
that if we have 370 Presidents of the United States;
or 370 Vice-Presidents; or 370 members of the Cabinet; or 370 leading Senators or Congressmen; or
370 generals and admirals; or 370 mayors of big
cities; or 370 governors of the states; or 370 other

high-ranking officials, we can be reasonably certain
that among each of these groups there will be more
than one perpetrator of a crime against property.
And these ruling perpetrators commit their crimes
on a larger scale than the ordinary violators of the
property laws and regulations. The same can be
said, with slight modifications, about the high government officials of other democratic countries.
Though limited in their power, these ruling groups
still have much more power than the rank and file
of the citizens. According to the hypothesis that
power corrupts, this excessive power of democratic
rulers tends to lead the government strata to a higher
criminality than that of the ruled population.

If and when all the known (confirmed by the
court verdict) crimes against property committed by
the high-rank officials are roughly counted (without
counting a possibly still larger number of the hush-
hushed violations), their rates are found to be higher
than the rates for the same kind of crime of the total
(ruled) populations.

4. SECULAR POWER AND SANCTITY: ROMAN CATHOLIC POPES.

The correctness of the rule that secular, coercive
power tends to corrupt its holders is obliquely cor-
roborated by the significant fact that the lowest percentage of canonized saints among Roman Catholic
Popes was during the period when their secular
power and supremacy over the state rulers was at its
zenith. This is shown by the following table which
lists all Popes who have held office in ten groups of
25 each. These ten groups cover the span from 32

A.D. to 1823. 1823 is chosen because one hundred years is the usual time lapse for the elevation of a pope to sainthood.

Groups	Number of Popes	Number Canonized	Period	Years in Office	Average Years in Office
1	25	25	32-274 A.D.	242	9.6
2	25	24	275-498	223	8.8
3	25	11	498-657	159	6.3
4	25	12	657-827	170	6.4
5	25	3	828-931	103	4.1
6	25	0	932-1048	116	4.6
7	25	2	1049-1216	167	6.7
8	25	2	1216-1378	162	6.6
9	25	1	1378-1585	207	8.2
10	25	0	1585-1823	238	9.5
Total	250	80		1751	7.0

The table shows clearly several things. First, the highest percentage of popes elevated to sainthood (100 and 96 per cent) occurred when the Christian Church was mainly "the City of God," and "the Kingdom not of this world," when it was persecuted, and when its popes hardly had any secular power (the periods: 32-274 A.D. and 275-498 A.D.). Second, with the increase of secular power of the popes in the period 498-827, the per cent of saintly popes notably declines. Third, the per cent of saintly popes is lowest for the periods when the secular power of the popes was at its highest, and when the papacy claimed supremacy above the secular power of the rulers of the states and empires. Fourth, a decrease in the secular power of popes of the nineteenth and twentieth centuries and the renaissance of the Roman Catholic Church as a primarily spiritual and moral body, is already marked by the beatification of Pope Pius X in 1951. In a singular way these data support our thesis about the demoral-izing and corrupting effects of too great coercive power vested in an individual or a group of rulers, even when they are spiritual and moral leaders like the Popes.

5. CONCLUSION

All evidence seems to corroborate our three generalizations. In addition to their theoretical significance, these propositions have a direct practical bearing upon the present and the future of mankind. They indicate clearly the terrible dangers faced by mankind today if a handful of the top chiefs of the most powerful existing governments continue to hold in the hollow of their hands the cosmic power of the nuclear arms and energy and if these chiefs and the upper ranks of the governments remain on the same low level of morality and high level criminality as most high ranking rulers of governments have in the past. Our generalizations also suggest several ways of reconstructing the existing governments in order to improve their moral integrity and help in preventing a misuse of nuclear energy by present and future governments. Finally, the three propositions are helpful in understanding a most important change in the basic structure of the governments which is already under way and which is likely to grow rapidly if, in the interim, the existing rulers do not plunge mankind anew into a catastrophic world war.

CHAPTER IV

OTHER POWER ELEMENTS
WITHIN THE STATE

We have seen in the preceding chapter proofs that heads of state tend to be more criminal than the populations they rule. We have noted, too, that the greater their power and the more independent of public support, the more corrupt they seem to become. The last proposition we have proved is a corollary to the one just noted, that criminality of rulers decreases with limitation of their power until it may be no higher than that of the rank and file.

Let us now examine the facts in the case of the nominally less powerful groups which in fact rule many of the so-called democratic nations today.

1. CORRUPTION IN STATE AND CITY GOVERNMENT

The Seabury Investigations, a Joint Legislative Committee in New York State in 1930-31, and the U. S. Senate Crime Investigating Committee which began in 1951 have revealed how corruption has become a part of federal, state and local government. The Seabury Committee published some 92,000 pages of testimony relating to the state of New York. The following material is but a brief summary of the findings of the Committee.

The focus of political influence, in the main, arose from Tammany Hall, which has had a long history in the state of New York. From 1902 to 1924 Tammany Hall was ruled by Charles F. Murphy (1858-1924), who at one time owned and operated a chain of saloons in New York City. Later he became Dock Commissioner and then became the Tammany leader in 1902. The political power of Tammany Hall was graft. "Honest" graft was accepted openly — it included such items as "contributions" from interested citizens for candidates for public office, and cuts on public contracts, as well as protection payments for gambling and liquor establishments during prohibition. Dishonest graft was accepted only in secret, and included such items as the incomes from controlled or protected prostitution and narcotic rings, and cuts from extortion rings. Murphy left a fortune of $2 million when he died.

An example of "honest" graft is the half-million dollar printing scandal involving Clarence Heal, who sold a monopoly over all state and city printing contracts to his own company, the Burland Printing Company. One of Neal's associates, the notorious Frank Costello, paid almost one million dollars in back income taxes to New York and the U. S. without prosecution. His 500 slot machines in New York were protected by the Hall.

State boss Edward Jaeckle saved $154,506 in fees in five years, while working as collector of back taxes in Erie County, New York. James Walker, while mayor of New York and later, accepted an alleged $43,000 for granting taxi cab franchises in New York, and "earned" over a million dollars from other unexplained sources. In three years of Walker's administration, the city was billed for land bought for school sites at about thirteen times its value, at a total loss to the taxpayers of about $87 million. He was also involved in a milk racket in which the Secretary to the Health Commissioner received $90,000 one year for allowing a known gangster to pass below-standard cream through official channels.

George W. Olvany, who ran Tammany after Murphy's death until 1931, was a member of a law firm which profited to the amount of over $5 million while he held this post.

William J. Flynn as Commissioner of Public Works amassed nearly $1 million in personal gain by using his official connections advantageously.

Judge Theorfel in six years amassed $170,000 from his interest in the automobile agency from which county officials bought their cars.

Charles W. Culkin, at one time a Sheriff under the Hall, combined bootlegging and an electric lamp business with his official duties, to a profit of $2 million. He guaranteed dismissal of all violation writs against the buildings of his electrical customers.

Peter J. Curran managed to "earn" $662,000 as an under-sheriff in six years from 1925 to 1931.

Joseph Flaherty, an Assistant Deputy Sheriff, deposited $21,000 in four months in office while his salary was $2700 per year.

James J. McCormick, a Deputy City Clerk of New York City, claimed that the $385,000 he banked in his six years in office represented "gifts from bridegrooms." His boss, Michael J. Cruise, was able to bank $143,000 in the same period.

Harry C. Perry allowed his Chief Clerk's office to be used for a professional gambling center. This activity and "loans" from friendly contractors netted him $135,000 during his administration.

Judge Vitale accumulated about $125,000 in four official years, before being removed. The career of this man provides evidence of Judicial corruption. He was seen at a dinner given by Ciro Terranova, a notorious Chicago gangster, an affair at which all the guests except the Judge were robbed.

Judge Ewald was found to have paid $25,000 for his job, which gave him the opportunity before his forced resignation to amass a small fortune promoting wildcat stock.

Judge Vause, another wildcat stock promoter, made about a quarter of a million dollars before being imprisoned.

Judge Silberman was ousted from office for his dealings with John D. Weston, confessed bribetaker in vice cases in New York. Another Judge involved in this same business was Norris, a woman.

Judge Mancuso, and his associates McQuade, Simpson and Goodman all resigned quickly when their careers were put under investigation.

Jimmy Hines, another Tammany boss, made a direct sale of his political influence to a crime syndicate headed by the notorious "Dutch" Schultz and "Dixie" Davis. This same Hines admitted publicly on one occasion that these gangsters had a large part in naming and electing the District Attorney.

The manner in which the Tammany ring stayed in power, besides its buying of influence and power was simply the stuffing of ballot boxes. The O'Connell ring, four brothers, dominated state politics in New York after 1921, and perfected a fraudulent system of rigging the vote which tied up the entire state — this during the regimes of Smith, Roosevelt, and Lehman in New York. The vote recorded under this ring was consistently the highest in the country for years. Their system of punishing Republican registrants is revealed in their use of tax assessments as rewards to property owners who voted "right," and its efficiency is indicated by the 1938 registrations of only 6930 Republicans and 51,035 Democrats. It was under the O'Connells that such powerful interests as the New York Central Railroad received reductions on their tax assessments for as much as $1 million each year.

The Tammany and New York organization is probably the largest of the city rings, but it is typical of all of them. Several others well known may be examined briefly.

Atlantic City was the domain of Enoch (Nucky) Johnson. As county treasurer Johnson made a salary of $6,000 per year. By either an amazing budgeting system or some other means he managed to keep at least one mistress, four automobiles, and a house whose yearly rental was about five-sixths of his salary. The gambling joints, brothels and criminal syndicates catering to various sections of the vice trade brought him most of his income. When Johnson finally went to jail for tax evasion, it was established that he had accepted thousands in bribes and paid out more thousands. One of his henchmen, Joseph Corio, himself collected a bribe of $60,000 for his influence, and later was given a judgeship. It was established that Johnson ran the city elections by the use of fraudulent registration rolls, ballot box stuffing, and imported "floaters" from Philadelphia.

In Jersey City, New Jersey, Frank Hague established a voting machine which was considered unbeatable. Hague managed to live as a millionaire for years on a salary of $8,000.

In Kansas City, Missouri, Thomas Pendergast held politics under his thumb for years. Pendergast's concrete and liquor companies netted him a fortune, since any public building erected in the city had to be built with his concrete or remain in blueprint. He controlled the liquor distribution monopoly by the same strongarm means. Prostitution was organized by him on a percentage basis. The registration lists of the city showed some 60,000 ghost names when investigated. Otto Higgins, Pendergast's Chief of Police, received a salary of $10,000 per month from the underworld for protecting prostitution and narcotics industries in and around Kansas City. Pendergast himself was finally sent to jail for tax evasion on a $315,000 bribe he took for swinging a decision in favor of some insurance firms to the detriment of their policy holders to the amount of $9 million.

Generally, no big city is free of similar organizations and syndicates, nor is any state. Large scale crime organization can *only* flourish with official protection and cooperation, and hence the professional criminal is always knocking on the door of the politician; he has more often than not been a welcome guest. It is unnecessary to multiply detailed examples.

A brief summary of some highlights suffices to demonstrate the fact that America has not been free of the vice of governmental corruption from the beginning and, indeed, suggests strongly that little important criminality of any organized nature has ever existed *except* in connection with the government and its personnel.

A somewhat similar situation has existed in other countries where the provincial, county, and city officials have had legal or factual opportunity to acquire considerable extra-legal power and to misuse it for their personal unlawful purposes. In such countries not only the high ranks of the government but a large portion of its middle and lower ranks seem to be more corrupt than the rank and file of comparable, ruled populations. In the countries where — through the civil service requirements, strict legal control, and strongly integrated public opinion — the middle and lower ranks of officialdom are greatly limited in their power and have an insignificant opportunity to acquire any considerable extra-legal power, these officials may actually be less criminal than the common population. This explains why in pre-war Germany, England, and some other nations, the criminality rate for government officials as a body was not higher than that for the total population, and was even lower than that for the population gainfully employed in industry, trade, mining, transportation, and agriculture. Since the bulk of civil service officials was strictly limited in power, and since the socio-cultural conditions gave little opportunity for the extra-legal increase of their power, the body of the middle and lower ranks of

the government personnel was as virtuous as the
common population.

2. CRIMINALITY OF CAPTAINS OF FINANCE AND INDUSTRY, LABOR LEADERS, AND OTHERS

If power tends to corrupt, then shall we expect
more crimes against property, more non-murderous
crimes against person, more sex-offences and other
lighter crimes among executives of big business and
finance, the manipulators that are go-betweens of
business and government, the leaders of big labor
unions and other powerful organizations? In an
economically-minded society like ours the big executives of wealth, industry, and labor are, as a rule,
powerful, sometimes even more powerful than the
rulers of the states who are often the puppets of these
leaders of industry, wealth, and labor.

The facts seem to confirm this expectation. In
regard to the captains of finance and wealth, it was
said long ago that it is easier for a camel to pass
through the eye of a needle than for the rich to enter
the Kingdom of God. The truth of this maxim is
well confirmed by the experience of the past as well
as by the careful histories of the modern big fortunes
and by the biographies of recent captains of industry
and finance, go-betweens, and some labor leaders.[1]
These histories and biographies show that in recent
times, just as in the past, there are few, if any, big
fortunes amassed without crime, just as there are few
captains of industry and finance, and few powerful
labor leaders that are free from criminal violations
of law and morality.

In the first place, it is these same captains, go-betweens, and labor leaders that initiate bribery and corruption of the government officials and often, when the lawful ways are unavailable, try to bypass the law to achieve their morally questionable purposes. John J. Astor, for one year's "services," gave $35,000 to Lewis Cass, among his briberies of various officials. Many government officials were bribed and corrupted by Morris Ketchum, Charles Huntington, Mark Hopkins, Charles Crocker, Leland Stanford, James J. Hill, James Fisk, Jay Gould, J. P. Morgan, E. H. Harriman, John D. Rockefeller, Andrew Carnegie, and other big business leaders. This continues up to the present day.

Besides bribing and corrupting government officials, big executives have committed other crimes against property, person, and the state. Their share in embezzlement and fraud seems to be much greater than the share of the rank and file. Already in 1895, A. R. Barrett showed that banks suffer more losses from skilled financiers than from the ordinary bank robbers.[2] R. T. Wood of the Fidelity Department of the American Surety Company reveals that "the total amount of embezzlement each year is variously estimated at from $200,000,000 to $405,000,000."[3] The greatest part of this total sum is made up of big embezzlements by businessmen like:[4] vice-president of a Texas bank who took $120,000; or a former U. S. Attorney sentenced for 10 years for misapplying large bank funds; or the Kentucky bankers charged with embezzlement of $2,000,000 and misapplication of $7,000,000; or an Illinois county auditor who took $65,000 and then committed suicide; or a manager in a Chicago bank who took $3,500,000 and was sentenced for 10 to 100 years; or the Kansas City manager indicted for embezzling $365,000; or a secretary-manager of a Building and Loan Association who for 8 years embezzled $10,811,000; and so on.

Passing over the large body of statistical data which can be found in the works mentioned, we include the following cases, which reveal the situation eloquently and are roughly typical. In 1923 ten leading industrialists and financiers held a much publicized meeting in the Edgewater Hotel in Chicago. For a number of years the American press has recounted the lives of these big business leaders. Those present were: Charles Schwab, president of the largest independent steel company in the U.S.A.; Basil Edmunds, president of the National City Bank of the United States; Samuel Insull, president of the largest utility holding company in the U.S.A.; Howard Hopson, president of a large gas company; Arthur Cutten, outstanding wheat speculator; Richard Whitney, president of the New York Stock Exchange; Albert Fall, a member of the U. S. Cabinet in the Harding administration; Jesse Livermore, a wealthy Wall Street broker; Ivar Kreuger, head of the Swedish Match Corporation; Leon Fraser, president of the Bank of International Settlement.

Twenty-five years later, in 1948, Schwab died in bankruptcy; Edmunds died of alcoholism in the slums of New York City, without funds; Insull died a fugitive from justice, without funds, outside of the United States; Hopson became insane and spent his last 15 years in the mental hospital where he died;

Cutten died abroad, a pauper, buried with funds gathered from friends; Whitney was convicted of fraud and other crimes and sentenced to Sing-Sing Prison (later released); Fall was convicted in the Teapot Dome scandal and sent to prison (later released because of poor health); Livermore committed suicide; Ivar Kreuger committed suicide after his world-wide fraud ($405,000,000) was exposed; and Leon Fraser committed suicide.

Of these 10 big business leaders four were involved in fraudulent dealings, and either were sent to prison or committed suicide. In 1948, for the total population of the United States, there was one embezzlement and fraud per about 6,666 population. Among these business leaders we have one embezzlement and fraud per 2.5 persons. Of course, these comparisons are crude; nevertheless, they are roughly indicative.

F. Lundberg sums up the situation in saying that most of the wealthy American families have seen their family heads indicted and placed on trial for serious crimes or misdemeanors. "Unless one takes into consideration underworld circles, in no other social group can one find a parallel."[5]

This sort of gallery includes such names as John J. Astor, Cornelius Vanderbilt, J. P. Morgan, J. D. Rockefeller, James Fisk, E. H. Harriman, Ph. D. Armour, J. O. Armour, Jay Gould, George W. Perkins, E. T. Stotesbury, Thomas F. Ryan, as well as Anthony Brady, M. and D. Guggenheim, Harry F. Sinclair, E. L. Doheny, James J. Hill, the Mellons, the Du Ponts, J. D. Ryan, Henry Havermeyer, H. Clay Pierce, C. H. Dodge, and others.

Some of these executives bluntly confirm the situation. Col. Vanderbilt says: "You don't suppose that you can run a railway in accordance with the statute, do you?" A. B. Stikney said to J. P. Morgan and others in 1890: "I have the utmost respect for you gentlemen individually, but as railroad presidents, I would not trust you with my watch out of my sight." James M. Beck states: "Diogenes would have been hard put to it to find an honest man in the Wall Street which I knew as a corporation attorney." This is confirmed by Charles F. Adams: "One difficulty in railroad management lies in the complete absence of any high regard for commercial honesty." Finally, A. Carnegie, at the time of his retirement, at the age of 65 years, crisply summed up the situation: "The amassing of wealth is one of the worst species of idolatry, no idol more debasing. To continue much longer overwhelmed by business cares and with most of my thoughts wholly upon the way to make more money in the shortest time, must degrade me beyond the hope of permanent recovery." Very revealing also is John D. Rockefeller's education of his sons. "I cheat my boys every chance I get; I want them sharp. I trade with the boys and skin them and just beat them every time I can. I want to make them sharp." Exactly this method of sharp, predatory practices, of cheating, embezzling, circumventing and transgressing the inconvenient laws and replacing them by favoring ones, marks the activities of a much larger proportion of the captains of finance and industry than of the rank and file.

The level of criminality of the go-between of business and government is typified by the criminal-

ity of the twenty leading city-bosses from 1850 to
1925. They are: William M. Tweed of New York,
John Kelly of New York, James McManes of Phila-
delphia, Hugh McLaughlin of Brooklyn, Edward
Butler of St. Louis, Charles Murphy of New York,
W. Flinn of Pittsburgh, G. B. Cox of Cincinnati,
Albert A. Ames of Minneapolis, Richard Crocker of
New York, Martin Lomasey of Boston, Israel W.
Durham of Philadelphia, Ch. L. Magee of Pittsburgh, "Big Tim" Sullivan of New York, Roger Sullivan of Chicago, Martin Behrman of New Orleans,
Ab. Ruef of San Francisco, E. H. Vare of Philadelphia, Fred Lundin of Chicago, and George W.
Olvany of New York. Of these twenty big city-
bosses, four served time in prison and ten were involved in serious criminal litigation. Only six lived
their lives without coming into a sharp conflict with
the police and the courts.[6] In this sample, some 70
per cent of the city bosses were guilty of criminal
actions ranging from forgery to murder. Again, this
rate cannot be taken as typical for all the go-betweens or big executives. Nevertheless, if we decrease the rate ten, twenty, or even fifty times, it
still remains far above the given rates of crimes
against property for the total population of the
United States.

This conclusion can be backed up by hundreds
of similar facts: 1400 cases of windfall profits,
amounting to hundreds of millions, were appro-
priated in the forties by the corporations that had
built or invested in the Federal Housing Administration's rental housing. These cases turned up in 1954.
The fantastically profitable contracts were obtained

with the help of paid-for fishing trips organized by
the business contractors for the government officials;
these were provided, among other things, with party
girls (three for $400.00). Examine if you will the
case of the indictment of 214 internal revenue employees in 1954 of whom 100 were convicted, including the head tax-collector of the Federal government.[7] Or look into the indictments of 18 high
officials and seven corporations in February, 1954,
on charges of defrauding the government in surplus
ship deals. Or review the case of procurement of
girls from respectable families for a few hundred
dollars for the holidaying corporate executives and
rich customers by playboys of rich families. Or investigate the large number of charities organized for
a private profit. Or study the series of illegal enter-
prises and industries organized with a small invest-
ment for getting quick and strikingly high returns
(tax-cheating, narcotics, hijacking, counterfeiting,
prostitution, shoplifting, etc.), in which a number
of highly respectable businessmen and/or officials
have co-operated with the underworld of crime and
vice.

Senator Kefauver's Committee, the McCarthy-
Army hearings, and the hearings of Senator John
L. McClellan's Committee disclosed a vast body
of illegal actions, practices, and petty immorality
of businessmen, officials, and especially of the
czars of the labor unions. These hearings have
brought to light a large number of routine criminal
actions practiced by a number of powerful leaders
of labor unions: the practices of shakedown, extortion, embezzlement, fraud, bribery, theft, threats,

beating, hijacking, kidnapping, and coercing those who happen to be obstacles to the labor-bosses' enrichment and domination. When labor unions are weak and the power of their leaders greatly limited, they are practically free from graft, corruption, and other defects. As their power grows, the labor leaders assume a social position almost identical with that of the big business executives: even in their high salaries and emoluments they begin to "monkey" the captains of finance and business. Under these conditions, the czars of labor unions become as susceptible to crime as the government officials and business executives. For this reason the rate of criminality of powerful labor bosses has to be, and actually is, above that of the rank and file of the ordinary labor population.

With modification, these conclusions are again applicable to the big business executives and labor leaders of other countries. They are as subject to the corruptive influence of a coercive great power as are American businessmen and labor bosses.

CHAPTER V

NOBLE DECLARATIONS
AND IGNOBLE POLICIES
OF TODAY'S RULERS

A dispassionate observation of the preachings and practices of governments of the twentieth century clearly shows their complete failure in restraining the forces of death and destruction. Two world wars supplemented by a host of smaller wars, and two gigantic revolutions (the Chinese and the Russian) followed by a legion of other devastating revolutions, incontrovertibly attest to this failure. These international and civil wars have made this the bloodiest, most destructive, and most inhuman of the twenty-five centuries.[1] Not all these wars and revolutions were intentionally engineered by all the governments, nor are all the governments equally responsible for them. Such a theory of causation of wars and revolutions is naive and untenable. Regardless of their wishes, however, governments of this century have been unable to keep their armed forces from killing and mutilating millions of human beings, from turning thousands of cities and villages to ashes, and from blowing into smithereens practically all values, beginning with God and ending with the moral prestige and authority of the governments themselves. They also have failed to maintain internal order and prevent bloody strifes within their own countries.

True, this tragic failure has been due not only to the mental, moral, and social deficiency of the governments, but also to the militant activities of various pressure groups, explosive configurations of selfish interests, irrational passions of the masses, and other huge, anonymous, historical forces. However, the governments and their militant allies can in no way be exonerated from their responsibility for these catastrophes. The ruling groups generally, and particularly aggressive governments that deliberately start wars for personal or tribal purposes, still remain the incendiaries of international and civil conflagrations. The rulers, being the builders and controllers of armed forces and of the most powerful means of destruction, are the only authorities legally and factually entitled either to restrain or to unleash their armies, navies, and air armadas. As a rule, the gigantic armed machinery is brought into action by the explicit orders of the governments. Since the governments of this century either deliberately started or failed to prevent these Apocalyptic wars and bloodiest revolutions, they bear the main responsibility for these catastrophes. By their tragic failure they have demonstrated their incapacity to be the real guardians of peace, order, and harmonious progress.

Nor has the situation improved since the termination of the Second World War. The governments and their representatives in the United Nations daily assure the world of their unreserved dedication to peace, freedom, and universal brotherhood. Unfortunately, in their actual behavior and policies the ruling groups of both the American and the Soviet blocs of nations practice little of what they preach. The governments of both alliances have been busily engaged in cold and hot wars, the armaments race, and massive retaliation, with simultaneous preparations for an even more destructive and inhuman war.

Although more than fourteen years have elapsed since the armistice, there is no real peace, no mitigation of the cold war, and no decrease in the danger of the Third World War. Instead, both blocs have been progressively increasing military budgets, intensifying the armaments race, recruiting allies for wholesale murder, madly building military bases, and conducting other shortsighted military, economic, and political maneuvers, which result in the deterioration of freedom and the alienation of the inalienable rights of citizens of both alliances. We observe a progressive totalitarianization of even the democratic regimes with a concomitant increase in crime, mental disease, insecurity and weariness, not to mention taxes, costs of living, and the many other burdens imposed upon the populations of both blocs. Practically everything is being sacrificed to prepare for the expected apocalyptic war. And, what is worse, the ruling groups of both sides unblushingly declare their intention to use all the nuclear and bacteriological means of extermination in future wars.

In brief, the post-armistice governments of both blocs and the United Nations have accomplished little in the task of building a lasting universal peace or a stable, creative order in each of their nations and in the world. Instead, they have already exploded the Korean, the Indo-Chinese, the Middle East and other "police actions," in which a larger number of victims were killed and mutilated than in all the Napoleonic wars and the wars of the nineteenth century put together. The hands of the impotent and now defunct League of Nations at least remained free from the blood of war victims, but the hands of the United Nations are already saturated with the blood of millions of victims of the "police actions" sanctioned by it.

Today's governments have also dismally failed to maintain internal order in their own empires or populations by civilized and humanitarian means. Instead, they have used the cruelest, the most barbaric, and the most inhuman means of collective responsibility and hostages in the mass-extermination, torture, and destruction of innocent men and women, old and young, of whole regions, cities and villages. The rulers perpetrated these "crimes against humanity" to intimidate the rebels or the revolutionaries against the existing governments, whether in the colonies or in the mother country. The policies of the French government in Algeria, of the English government in Malaya, Cyprus, Yemen, and elsewhere, and of the Soviet government in Hungary, in Russia itself, and the satellite countries, the policies of the Formosan and the Chinese governments are examples of this bestial method of maintenance of order. Most governments in both blocs have carried out this sort of policy in a milder way in regard to their own or their colonial populations. The pity of all these savage policies is their uniform failure to achieve their task; instead of establishing peace and order, they have murdered and maimed thousands of innocent victims, destroyed many inhabited regions, and immeasurably increased anarchy and mutual hatred. If they liberated anything, it is only the worst of the beasts in thousands of human beings.

Intentionally or not, today's ruling groups have also contributed a great deal to the danger of explosion of a new world war, local wars, and bloody revolutions. At the moment of this writing, their airplanes are armed with atomic and hydrogen bombs and their missiles are fully triggered for momentary discharge of their deadly peace-content over millions of human beings. Finally, the ideologists of the governments are quite busy preparing the Gaither, the Rockefeller, and other "reports" demanding many additional billions from the impoverished taxpayers to carry on a still madder armaments race in preparation for a still more Satanic world war. Directly and indirectly, the ruling groups have uselessly wasted a cosmic amount of the world's natural resources and have not only squandered all of the accumulated wealth of mankind, but have piled up trillions in "national debts" to be paid by future generations. The guardians thus have succeeded in burdening not only living but also unborn generations with incalculable indebtedness.

The governments have also succeeded well in cultivating fear, distrust, and hatred by poisoning the neighborly relations of various nations and groups. By intensive training of millions of draftees and civil populations in the art of killing, by glorifying the "patriotic" extermination of all those who are not with us and those who are our opponents, the contemporary rulers have demoralized mankind, especially its young generations, more than any other agency.   The increase in juvenile delinquency is partially due to these policies.   The governments have also contributed to the disintegration of the greatest values, beginning with science and ending with religion, and of the greatest social institutions, beginning with the family and ending with the government itself.

By these policies, the present rulers have caused the death of millions of victims of their "police actions" and "brush-wars," notably harmed the physical and mental health of additional millions of the ruled populations, and planted the radioactive seeds of a potential degeneration of the human species on this planet.   These blind and irresponsible actions of those in power have robbed mankind of security, peace of mind, happiness, and creativity.

CHAPTER VI

WHO SHALL GUARD
THE GUARDIANS?

Who, then, shall guard the guardians? This age-old question has momentous significance in our time. Recent scientific discoveries have given us the nuclear and bacteriological means to exterminate the human race, civilization, and life itself on this planet. For the past few years these weapons have been manufactured on a gigantic scale by the governments of the United States, Soviet Russia, and Great Britain. At the present time, the number of these stockpiled weapons (and of the planes and missiles capable of carrying them) is sufficient to bring about the aforementioned calamity. And to compound calamity, other governments are now hastening to join this unholy armaments race!

The danger in this situation is intensified by the fact that this immense fund of deadly power is monopolistically controlled by a mere handful of governmental rulers, assisted by a few leaders of science and technology and the captains of industry and finance. In toto, the number of these guardians of the forces of death and destruction hardly exceeds a few hundred, and in the event of a tense international situation, the use or misuse of these forces is actually decided upon by a few dozens of these guardians. Thus today, the power which they hold is infinitely greater and more absolute than that of any of the monarchs, dictators, or military conquerors of the past. Coercive measures of governments, reinforced by the vast propaganda machinery at the disposal of the rulers, make it possible for these guardians to unleash this power with little difficulty, desolating cities and villages, poisoning the sources of our food and drink, killing hundreds of millions of people, mutilating unborn future generations, and even rendering this planet uninhabitable for most species of animals and plants. By comparison, the power of the absolute autocrats of the past was negligible, for they could destroy only a fraction of humanity. Under the present circumstances, should such a holocaust occur, life itself on this planet would hang in balance.

Thus, the question, *Quis custodiet ipsos custodes* (Who shall guard the guardians?) acquires a truly fateful importance. Can we be certain that the contemporary guardians of deadly power will never release it for the enforcement of their internal and international policies? Can we be sure that they have the necessary wisdom, moral responsibility, and mere common sense to abstain from starting what would prove to be the greatest catastrophe in human history? Do we have any real, foolproof guarantee against such madness in contemporary rulers? Despite a natural wish to answer these questions affirmatively, no cheerful answers are possible.

The preceding chapters have shown that the powerful ruling groups have been rather poor guardians of peace and moral order in the human universe. A large percentage of rulers have had either mediocre or low intelligence; many have also suffered from split personality, compulsive-obsessive complexes, aggressiveness, manias, paranoia, schizophrenia and other mental disorders. Morally, the ruling groups have been more criminal than the ruled populations. No wonder, therefore, that this kind of leader has been unable to secure for mankind any lasting peace or "life, liberty, and pursuit of happiness" in the preceding millennia of human history.

From 600 B.C. to A.D. 1959, during some twenty-five centuries of their guardianship, the incidence of war occurred, on an average, every two to four years, while the incidence of an important internal disturbance was about every five to seventeen years in the history of Greece, the Roman Empire, and eleven European and American nations. This is a poor record of these rulers as peacemakers and builders of internal order; and it is a very good record of these guardians as war-mongers and disturbers of internal stability of their nations. If such ruling groups have not been able to establish a lasting international and internal peace throughout man's past history, there is no reason to believe they can do so now.

The social and moral "spectrum" of the existing governments and of sociocultural conditions is sinister rather than reassuring. Most of the existing governments are totalitarian, autocratic, and dictatorial. Such are almost all the governments in the Soviet-Chinese bloc and a considerable portion of the ruling groups in the bloc of so-called free nations: the governments of Turkey, Formosan China, both Vietnams, both Koreas, Spain, Thailand, Iraq, Iran, Saudi Arabia, Jordan, several Latin-American governments, etc. The United Nations does not and cannot materially improve this situation because its delegates are but the spokesmen of the existing governments. Still more important is the fact that the great governments now possess nuclear arms and energy, the monopolistic control of which makes them uniquely powerful. Since power tends to corrupt, the contemporary "nuclear" governments can hardly avoid this corruption. The demoralizing effect of the gigantic power they hold is reinforced by the factors of interminable cold wars, local hot wars, and by the various emergencies of our times, such as famine, depression, revolts, epidemics, floods, droughts, earthquakes, etc., that indefatigably sweep over tired humanity. As shown elsewhere,[2] these factors tend to make governments increasingly totalitarian. Nor have the existing democratic regimes escaped this increase of totalitarian tendencies during the last decades. After the armistice they greatly decreased their war-time totalitarianism, but under the influence of these factors, they have been gradually reconverting back toward totalitarianism, autocracy, and limitation of the inalienable rights and liberties of their citizens and private groups.

This dangerous situation is still further aggravated by the prevailing social, mental, and moral anarchy of our age. The previous system of basic values is now largely disintegrated, but a new system of values has not yet been built. Hence, the extraordinary confusion that prevails in our hearts, minds, and souls. Hence, also, the conspicuous lack of any unified public opinion of the world which might effectively guide and control contemporary men and women, and especially the existing governments and rulers. A multitude of mutually contradictory opinions of diverse factions is a poor substitute for the real, unified public opinion of mankind. None of the "pseudo-public opinions" of these cliques can effectively prevent governments from starting a new world war or committing other acts of catastrophic insanity; nor can they powerfully inspire the existing ruling groups to the acts of sublime morality and heroic creative achievements. In this anarchy, the governments are much more free from the control of mankind's conscience than they would be if a well integrated, universal system of values were functioning; in this "disorganized dust of individuals" there is no common conscience to support sound actions.

The sinister constellation of these factors does not give any guarantee against the misuse of this deadly nuclear power by its contemporary guardians. If anything, the constellation portends rather the misuse and abuse of this power by the existing rulers and their henchmen. Upon close analysis, most of these guardians, like those of the past governments, appear to be shortsighted rather than wise, moved by selfish interests rather than moral imperatives of mankind's well-being. So far their policies of peace-making have been fruitless. If the rulers (and the ruled) are not brought under the control of the wisest, most creative, and most moral forces, the outlined record of the governments and of the prevalent sociocultural situation does not warrant any optimism at this, the most crucial moment of human history.

But can the rulers, the ruled, and the critical sociocultural conditions be brought under such a control? And if so, what immediate steps are necessary to prevent the explosion of a new world war, to make the governments wiser and less criminal, and to change respectively the ruled population and the existing critical sociocultural conditions?

Only an omniscient superman can answer these questions infallibly. Unfortunately, we can offer only hypotheses and suggestions. Since some of these questions are discussed and answered elsewhere,[3] there is no reason to repeat the analyses here. In this essay we offer only the ideas that directly concern the problem of how to make the rulers and governments less criminal, less destructive, and less short-sighted, or, positively, how to make them more creative, constructive, and morally ennobled.

Chapter VII

PREVENTING A NEW
WORLD WAR

It is necessary, first of all, to state that the following suggestions are to be regarded as short-term emergency measures. Taken alone, they can be only partially successful for a very limited time. To be fully successful over an indefinitely long period, these emergency measures must be supplemented and reinforced by a much more basic reconstruction of mankind's systems of values, culture, and social institutions — by the transformation of man himself. This basic reconstruction requires a much longer time and far greater effort on the part of all than the mere limitation of the power of rulers, but only such a reconstruction can prevent future catastrophes and improve both the rulers and the ruled. We will not analyze the process completely here,[1] for the following propositions are primarily concerned with the wisdom and morality of governments and the prevention of future wars.

1. *Since power tends to corrupt, the power of the existing autocratic and democratic-governments which possess the monopolistic control of nuclear arms and energy must be greatly limited, if we want to improve the moral integrity of the governments.*

2. *The same is to be done with the extra-legal and autocratic power of the captains of industry and finance, the top executives of big corporations, the bosses of big labor unions, and of any person who holds an unduly great coercive power.*

3. *This limitation of power is to be brought about in an orderly manner, without physical violence, mainly through scientific and moral persuasion and according to due process of law.*

4. *The limitation of the rulers' power must not, however, be so drastic as to leave mankind and each nation without protection against the crimes of individuals and gangs.*

If too much power corrupts, a lack of power is still worse, for it leads to anarchy and to war of everyone against everybody.

There is only one way to decrease drastically the dangerous power of nuclear governments and to prevent them from starting a new world catastrophe, namely: *universal, total disarmament* (leaving a small police force for coping with criminals and the socially dangerous insane). Partial disarmament in whatever form cannot serve the purpose, because it still leaves a vast power in the hands of the governments. Neither legally nor factually does it inhibit the rulers from starting so-called limited or "brush-wars." Once started, a "brush-war" can easily develop into a world-conflagration. As we have seen at the present time there are no reliable agencies or forces which can with certainty prevent such a development. The existing governments and their ruling associates are entirely unreliable in this matter. Nor do contemporary atomization of the basic values and the prevailing mental, moral, and social anarchy afford us any grounds for optimism. If anything, the low moral standards of the rulers and this anarchy offer serious doubt that the existing governments will resist the temptation of using all available means of war, especially if heavily pressed by the enemy. We must keep in mind that the use of the nuclear and equally destructive arms by just one government or ruler is quite sufficient to transform a brush-war into a world-conflagration; all the other governments will immediately follow the example and retaliate by using the same destructive war instruments. In this way the limited war can easily become the unlimited one.

To assume that, of the hundreds of the existing governments and totalitarian rulers, not one will succumb to this temptation is a most improbable assumption. The experience of the last two World Wars showed that even such powerful democratic governments as the Truman administration already used atomic weapons, strategic bombing, and practically every sort of arms available. The oft-mentioned abstention from using poisonous gas does not prove the opposite; the little use of this weapon is due, not to the moral scruples of the governments or to their mutual fear of retaliation, but to the poor controllability of the gas itself. Air currents and winds sometimes caused it to blow over the population and army of the gas-using government instead of those of the enemy. With the present increase in the controllability and deadliness of poisonous gases, practically all governments are arming themselves with this weapon, and are clearly going to use it in the next wars.

These and similar considerations should suffice to explain why any partial disarmament cannot prevent the conflagration of a new world-war. The persons and rulers who believe in the salutary limited "brush-wars" or in the possibility of a lasting peace under the conditions of a partial disarmament are expecting miracles which are impossible in our schizophrenic world. Only total, universal disarmament reinforced by the basic reconstruction of man's personal, social, and cultural house can give to man lasting peace and harmonious life. Now, to turn to the meaning of this total, universal disarmament. It means:

First, the unconditional outlawing of war as a means for settling international or intranational conflicts, by each and all governments as well as the United Nations. This outlawing implies: a) a solemn unconditional prohibition of all kinds of war by the United Nations; b) an amendment to the constitution of each government, depriving that government of the right to declare, or to carry on a war (this prohibition also refers to all kinds of civil war); c) another amendment to the constitutions declaring freedom from military service as the inalienable right of every person.

Second, the destruction or conversion into peaceful instruments of all existing arms of all countries.

Third, cessation of manufacturing of all kinds of armament (particularly the nuclear, bacteriological, and other destructive war-means) in all countries and by all governments.

Fourth, total de-mobilization and disbanding of all armed forces in all countries and prohibition of all sorts of military recruitment (voluntary or coercive) for the rebuilding of new armed forces.

Fifth, the complete elimination of all kinds of military ranks, military schools, and other ways of training armed forces and war specialists.

Sixth, eliminating from the budget of every country all military appropriations (except some pensions and economic help to the retired military personnel and veterans).

Seventh, the enactment by all governments of a law-statute making the actions of inciting, preparing, and starting international or civil war a criminal and punishable felony.

Such measures not only legally prohibit wars of all kinds, but they eliminate war factually by radically depriving all governments of the means and personnel with which to start and to wage any war-activity. Without such means, even the wickedest rulers could not plunge mankind into a bloody catastrophe.

Eighth, the great task of total, universal disarmament can and should be materially fostered by all true religious, ethical, philosophical, scientific, educational, political, artistic, labor, farmer, and business organizations. If their members want to survive, if they do not want the end of man's creative mission on this planet, if the organizations and leaders want peace and the harmonious growth of their creative work, they are bound to exert all their efforts toward the realization of lasting peace, by ennobling the government morally and implementing total and universal disarmament as the necessary steps toward these objectives.

If all such organizations begin to work earnestly

for these great causes, they can radically change the total moral and mental climate of mankind in a comparatively short time. Using all the means of communication and all the effective methods of moral and mental re-education,[2] these organizations can make the very idea of murder so utterly repulsive (intellectually as well as emotionally) as to render the perpetration of such an act impossible for an overwhelming majority of human beings.

These considerations also apply to the task of reducing the unmerited, extra-legal, and irresponsible portion of the power of the autocratic political rulers, the executives of big corporations, the dictatorial bosses of labor unions, and the too-bossy or -foxy leaders of other powerful organizations. The time for autocratic, absolutistic, morally and legally irresponsible, selfish, and creatively mediocre leaders is running out in practically all constructive, creative, and beneficial organizations. With very few exceptions, mankind no longer needs this sort of leaders. They have outlived their usefulness and should now be replaced by more intelligent, more creative, and more moral leadership.

Chapter VIII

THREE BASIC TRENDS
OF OUR TIME

The beginnings of such a replacement are already noticeable at the present time. Although on the surface of mankind's social life the trends towards more cynical, totalitarian, and coercive governments seemingly still prevail, in the deeper layers of today's historical reality new beginnings and trends have already emerged. They are bound to grow rapidly if mankind does not commit suicide. The "new beginnings and trends" in the nature of rulership and governments are but a part of a much greater change in the whole character of the existing culture, social organization, and type of human personality. We must briefly outline this epochal change to understand correctly the new trends in political institutions and governments.

1. The Crisis in Western Society

Some thirty years ago a detailed analysis of this change was made containing forecasts of the coming trends, including repeated warnings about the immediate terrible wars, bloody revolutions, misery, and "liberation" of the worst of the beasts in man.[1] In a summarized form this diagnosis and prognosis run as follows:

Every important aspect of the life, organization and the culture of Western society is in the extraordinary crisis. . . . Its body and mind are sick.

116

. . . We are seemingly between two epochs: the dying Sensate (Secular) culture of our magnificent yesterday and the coming (new) culture of the creative tomorrow. We are living, thinking and acting at the end of a brilliant six-hundred-year-long Sensate day. The oblique rays of the sun still illumine the glory of the passing epoch. But the light is fading, and in the deepening shadows it becomes more and more difficult to see clearly and to orient ourselves safely in the confusions of the twilight. The night of the transitory period begins to loom before us, with its nightmares, frightening shadows and heartrending horrors. Beyond it however the dawn of a new great culture is probably waiting to greet the men of the future.[2]

Despite inimical criticism of this diagnosis by the gaudily optimistic opinion of the 1920s, the past 30 years have proven it to be correct. Briefly, the main aspects of this crisis are as follows:

The Sensate form of culture, which has been dominant in the Western world during the last five centuries is disintegrating. The crisis involves all compartments of this Sensate culture and society and is, therefore, the greatest of all the crises of the Western world's history.

Sensate Culture. The Sensate form of culture and society is based upon the ultimate principle that the true reality and value are sensory, and that beyond the reality and values which we can perceive through our sense-organs there are no others. The whole system of Sensate culture represents mainly an articulation and materialization of this ultimate principle in Sensate culture's science and philosophy, its modicum of religion, its law and ethics, its economics

and politics, its fine arts and social institutions. This
basic principle becomes also the main determinant of
the dominant mentality, aspirations, and way of life
of Sensate society. Quite consistently with this principle, Sensate culture makes the testimony of our
senses the criterion of what is true and what is false.
It intensely cultivates scientific knowledge of the
physical and biological properties of sensory reality,
and is relatively uncreative in the field of religion,
ethics, and theology.

Sensate society is also quite successful in making
a legion of technological inventions aimed at increasing the bodily comforts of sensory life, but has
little success in transfiguration of souls and in attaining the perennial and universal supersensory
values of the Supreme Truth, Goodness, and Beauty.
It greatly favors the development of materialist,
empiricist, positivist and other sensory philosophies,
and inhibits the cultivation of idealistic, mystical and
supersensory systems of philosophy. Despite its lip-
service to the values of the Kingdom of God, it cares
mainly about the sensory values of wealth, health,
bodily comfort, sensual pleasures, power, and fame.
Its dominant ethic is invariably utilitarian and hedonistic. It views all ethical and legal precepts as
mere man-made conventions, perfectly relative and
changeable. Its politics and economics are also decisively utilitarian and hedonistic. Its government is
secular, consisting of statesmen and politicians, beginning with the hereditary or elective chief of state and
ending with the little ward-politicians and policemen.
The power of these secular governments is based
either upon wealth, force, or upon election and utili-

tarian services of the politicians to the electorate which represents either a small oligarchic faction, or a vast body of citizens who in their turn are often but a small group superimposed upon the still larger bodies of slaves, serfs, and colonial peoples. With few exceptions, the bulk of the politician-rulers are neither competent experts in any important field nor complete ignoramuses in many fields.

Sensate fine arts are marked by similar sensory characteristics. Sensate form emerged in Western culture at the end of the twelfth century; it subsequently grew and, after the fifteenth century, became dominant, supplanting the preceding Religious or Ideational culture which had dominated the Mediaeval period of Western culture and society from about the seventh to the thirteenth century.

Ideational Culture. The Ideational culture of the Middle Ages was based upon the ultimate principle that the true reality and value is the supersensory and superrational God and His Kingdom as defined in the Christian *Credo*. Therefore, sensory reality and value is either a mirage or even something negative and sinful. Quite consistently with this principle, this culture believes in God's revelations rather than in the testimony of our senses as the criterion of truth. Accordingly, Ideational culture cares little about scientific study of sensory phenomena and technology; since the whole sensory world is merely a mirage, such activities are but a waste of time and energy dealing with the shadows of reality and value.

For this reason, Ideational culture is uncreative in the field of science and technology. Instead, it concentrates its cognitive energy on a study of the

Kingdom of God and a realization of its values in the short, earthly pilgrimage to eternity. St. Augustine's *Deum et animam scire cupio. Nihilne plus? Nihil omnino* (I want to know God and Soul. Nothing more? Absolutely nothing.) admirably expresses this aspect of Ideational culture. Therefore, it is creative in the field of religion; theology logically becomes the queen of science, and science functions only as the handmaid of religion. Only idealistic, mystical and supersensory philosophies blossom in it, for it aspires mainly for the salvation of souls and the values of God's Kingdom, and views as sin and temptation an excessive care for material and sensory values. Its verities, ethical and legal precepts, are regarded as God's revealed commandments, universal and unconditional in their truth and binding power. Its government is conspicuously theocratic and its spiritual authority has supremacy over the secular powers. Its economics is conditioned by its religious and moral commandments.

Finally, Sensate and Ideational cultures have entirely different types of fine arts, each created in accordance with the ultimate principle of the culture and differing from the other in subject matter as well as in style.

Integral Culture. Once in a while, a third— the Integral—type of culture, an intermediary between the Sensate and the Ideational, appears and blossoms for a comparatively short time. Its ultimate principle proclaims that the true reality-value is an Infinite Manifold in which the supersensory, rational and sensory forms are inseparable from one another.

Eclectic Culture. Finally, there is the Eclectic—

unintegrated or disintegrated—culture which never becomes a great culture.

Each of these types of culture has been realized several times in history: among pre-literate tribes, in Ancient Egypt, Babylon, Iran, India, China, Greece and Rome, and the Western world.

Respectively, the three greatest trends of our time are: (1) a continued disintegration of the hitherto dominant Sensate culture, society and system of values; (2) the emergence and slow growth of the first components of a new Integral dominant order and system of values; (3) a shift of the creative leadership of mankind from Europe and the European West, where it has been centered during the last five centuries, to a wider area of the Pacific and the Atlantic, particularly the Americas, Asia, and Africa.

2. SHIFT IN CREATIVE LEADERSHIP

In the past, for millennia, the creative torch of mankind was carried on mainly by the Asiatic and the African peoples. While our European forefathers had still a most primitive culture and way of life, in Asia and Africa a number of great civilizations emerged, grew up, and then either declined or fluctuated. Such were the great cultures of Ancient Egypt, Sumer, Babylon, Iran, India, China, Creto-Mycenae, Ancient Greece and Rome, which were Mediterranean civilizations rather than European, and of the Arabic world. It is only for the last five centuries or so that the European peoples (in Europe and on other continents) have almost monopolistically carried on the torch of creative

progress in science, technology, philosophy, Sensate
arts, economics, and politics. Now this monopolistic
European leadership is about at an end. The main
stars of the next acts of the great drama of human
history are going to be the peoples and cultures of
the Americas, India, China, Russia, Japan, the
Arabic world, and Europe. However, from now on
the European and the Euro-American or Western
culture and peoples will no longer be the only stars
or the only bearers of the torch of creativity, but
merely members of the galaxy, and not necessarily
the greatest among them.

This great shift of the creative center of human
history has already progressed so much as to become
noted by some of the shrewd politicians and by
thoughtful observers of the East and the West. The
shift is pregnant with momentous changes in all compartments of all cultures and societies, including the
area of political regimes and governments. This shift
is already causing many transformations in the
structure, personnel, and the functions of the existing
ruling *elite*.

3. Sociocultural Trends

The other two basic social trends of our time
consist of: a) a progressive decay of the hitherto
dominant Sensate culture, society, and man, and
b) of an emergence and slow growth of the first
components of the new — possibly Integral — sociocultural order and man.

This epochal struggle between the progressively
sterile and destructive forces of the dying Sensate
order and the creative forces of the emerging, Inte-

gral, sociocultural order marks all compartments of today's cultural and social life and deeply affects the ways of life of every one of us.

In *science* this double process has manifested itself on the one hand, in: a) an increasing destructiveness of the morally irresponsible, Sensate scientific achievements such as the nuclear means of warfare invented and continuously perfected by Sensate scientists; on the other, b) in an increasing number of scientists who refuse to cooperate in this destructive misuse of science and scientific creativity, in an establishment and growth of scientific organizations like our Society for Social Responsibility in Science, and, finally, in a transformation of the basic theories of science in a morally responsible, Integral, direction.

Physical Sciences. This change has already made today's science less materialistic, mechanistic, and deterministic—or less Sensate—than it was during the preceding two centuries. For this modern science matter has become but a condensed form of energy which dematerializes into radiation. The material atom is already dissolved into more than thirty non-material, cryptic, arcane, perplexing, enigmatic, and inscrutable elementary particles: the electron and the anti-electron, the proton and the anti-proton, the photon, the mesons, etc., or into the image of waves which turn out into the waves of probability, waves of consciousness which our thought projects afar. These waves like those associated with the propagation of light quanta need no substratum in order to propagate in space-time; they undulate neither in fluid, nor in solid, nor yet in a gas. Around a bend of quantum mechanics and at the foot of the electronic ladder the basic notions of materialistic and mechanistic science such as: matter, objective reality, time, space, causality are no longer applicable, and the testimony of our senses largely loses its significance. As to the deterministic causality, it is already replaced in the modern science by Heisenberg's principles of uncertainty, by fanciful "quanta jumps," by a mere chance relationship or—in psychosocial phenomena—by voluntaristic, free-willing, law of direction exempt from causality and chance.

Biological, Psychological and Social Sciences. Similar transformations have taken place in the new, leading theories of biological, psychological, and social sciences. In contrast to the superannuated, though still intoned, cliches of mechanistic, materialistic, and deterministic biology, psychology, and sociology, the rising, significant theories in these disciplines clearly show that the phenomena of life, organism, personality, mind, and sociocultural processes are irreducible to, and cannot be understood as, purely materialistic, mechanistic, and sensory realities. According to these theories they have, besides their empirical aspect, the far more important mindfully-rational and even supersensory and superrational aspects. In these and other forms the most modern science has already become notably Integral in comparison to what it was in the nineteenth century. This means an increasing replacement of the dying Sensate elements of science by the new—Integral—ones.

This replacement becomes clear if we take a few basic problems in physical, biological, and social sciences. We can begin with the problem of the *true and total reality*. As mentioned before, Sensate science of preceding centuries explicitly and implicitly tended to reduce this reality either to matter or to the sensory reality as it is perceived by our sense organs. Such a science either denied or had an agnostic attitude toward any non-sensory reality. At the present time this conception of reality is already largely abandoned by all sciences as too narrow and inadequate. It is already superseded by an incomparably wider and more adequate conception of the total reality. Today this total reality is thought of as the infinite X of numberless qualities and quantities: spiritual and material, temporal and timeless, everchanging and unchangeable, personal and superpersonal, spatial and spaceless, one and many. In this sense it is conceived as the veritable *coincidentia oppositorum, mysterium tremendum et fascinosum*. Of its innumerable modes of being, three basic forms appear to be important: a) empirical-sensory, b) rational-mindful, and c) superrational-supersensory. The new conception does not deny the sensory form of reality, but it makes it only one of its three main aspects. This new conception of the true reality, being incomparably richer and more adequate than the old one, is at the same time much nearer to the true and total reality of practically all great religions, especially of their mystical currents.

In accordance with this change, *the scientific theory of cognition of the true reality* has greatly changed also. Though a few voices still intone John Locke's classical formula: *Nihil esse in intellectu quod non fuerit prius in sensu* and monotonously repeat the old refrain that sensory perception and observation is the only avenue to scientific cognition and knowledge, this theory of cognition is already obsolescent and is largely replaced by a more adequate theory corresponding to the new conception of the total reality. According to this new—Integral—theory of knowledge, we have not one but at least three different channels of cognition: sensory, rational, and supersensory-superrational. The empirical aspect of the total reality is perceived by us through our sense organs and their extensions: microscopes, telescopes, etc. The rational aspect of the reality is comprehended by us mainly through our reason: mathematical and logical thought in all its rational forms. Finally, the glimpses of the super-rational-supersensory forms of the reality are given to us by the true supersensory-superrational intuition, or divine inspiration, or flash of enlightenment of all creative geniuses: founders of great religions, sages, seers, and prophets, giants of philosophy and ethics, great scientists, artists, moral leaders and other eminent creators in all fields of culture. These geniuses unanimously testify the fact that their discoveries and creation of their masterpieces have been started and then guided by grace of intuition quite different from sensory perception or logico-mathematical reasoning. All the great discoveries and masterpieces in all fields of culture have always been inspired by this intuition and then developed and tested through its cooperation with the other two — sensory and rational — ways of cognition and creativity.[3]

The acknowledgement of the important role of the superrational-supersensory intuition in cognition and creativity by the new—Integral—theory represents a confirmation and a more precise formulation of an old, basic idea of practically all great religions and of many great philosophies exemplified by such concepts as: the supersensory-superrational Tao, "no-knowledge" or "eternal reason" in Taoism; prajna and jnana and the states of samadhi and zatori, in Hinduism and Buddhism; the "enlightenment," "the illumination," "the divine revelation" and "the inner light," in Christianity and other religions; "divine madness" in Plato's and in other "mystic" systems of philosophy. In this point the new Integral system appears again as more congenial to religious ideas about the supersensory-superrational sources and forms of cognition and creativity than the old Sensate theory of knowledge and creativity.

The same can be said of the old Sensate and the new—Integral—*theory of human personality and of human mind.* The Sensate theories viewed man mainly as an animal organism of the *homo sapiens* species. They tended to interpret his nature and behavior predominantly in mechanistic, materialistic, reflexological, and other "physicalistic" terms. Some of these Sensate theories have even denied the reality of the human mind. Some others saw in it only two forms of mental energy: unconscious (or subconscious, or preconscious) and conscious. The recent decadent form of Sensate theories, exemplified by S. Freud's yarns, largely reduced mind or human psyche to the pan-sexual unconscious libido or id, with epiphenomenal ego and superego representing a modification of the same unconscious under the pressure of the family and society's censorship. This sort of Sensate theory of personality represents but a decadent and atrocious variety of the previous, more sound Sensate conceptions of man. In the Freudian and similar recent conjectures the distortion and degradation of human nature reached its lowest level.

Fortunately, an increased knowledge of human personality has led to an essential repudiation of these decadent Sensate theories as fantasmagoric scientifically, ugly aesthetically, and demoralizing ethically, and to an emergence and growth of the new—more scientific and adequate—conceptions in this field. In these new theories man is conceived as a marvelous integral being. He appears to be not only an animal organism but also a rational thinker and doer; in addition, he proves to be a supersensory and superrational being, an active and important participant in the supreme, creative forces of the cosmos. He is not only an unconscious and conscious creature, but he is especially a superconscious master-creator capable of controlling and transcending his unconscious and conscious energies in the moments of his divine inspiration, in the periods of his highest and intensest creativity. As mentioned, man's greatest discoveries and creative achievements have been largely due to man as the superconscious master-creator, assisted by man as a rational thinker and by man as an empirical observer and experimenter. If man were only an organism, motivated and guided only by the libidinal or other forms of the unconscious, he would have had as little chance to become the highest creative agent in the total universe as other biological species endowed only with the reflexological-

instinctive unconscious and with the rudiments of the
conscious mind. Exactly, the endowment of *homo
sapiens* with a developed rational mind and with the
superconscious genius is responsible for a truly as-
tounding and ever-growing creativity of man. As we
see, this new—Integral—theory of human personality
again appears to be quite congenial to the religious
idea of man as a son of God, created in the image
of the Supreme Creator. This triadic theory of
personality is a more precise formulation of the
triadic conceptions of man prevalent in great religions. These conceptions viewed man as a triadic
creature having three forms of being: a) the unconscious (reflexo-instinctive mechanism of body),
b) the conscious (rational mind), and c) the supra-
conscious creator ("Nous," "Pneuma," "Spirit,"
"Soul," "Divine Self"). In the rational and the superconscious properties of man lies the answer to the
ancient question: "What is man, that thou shouldst
magnify him?"

As a further example of the struggle between
the decaying Sensate and the emerging new—
Integral—theories and practices, we can take the
problem of the *main factors of biological evolution
of the species, of human behavior, and of mental,
moral, and social progress of mankind.* The Sensate
—biological, psychological, and sociological—theories of the nineteenth and of the twentieth centuries
have viewed the struggle for existence as the main
factor of evolution of the species and of human
progress. The Freudian and other recent variations
of these theories considered the sex and the hateful
destructive — sadistic and masochistic — instincts as

the main factors of human behavior. Economics and other social disciplines have been based upon the postulate of the egotistic man, motivated entirely by his selfish interests and relentlessly pursuing these objectives in all forms of deadly rivalry and milder competition.

These Sensate beliefs are still daily reiterated in the mottoes like: "It is rivalry and competition that made America great," "the struggle for existence is the supreme law of life," "for protection of our national interests all means of warfare, including the nuclear ones, are perfectly just and right," and so on.

These Sensate beliefs have been unblushingly implemented and have resulted in the genocydal total wars and revolutions of this century with their mass-murders of not only millions of the combatants, but also of the non-combatants, including children, women and the old folk; into a wholesale destruction of cities and vastly populated regions; into the mad armament race and preparations for the next— nuclear and bacteriological—total wars unrestrained by human or divine laws. In these and similar ways the partisans of these Sensate theories, especially the governments of the mighty nations, have openly declared themselves free from all restraints of international law and all the moral precepts of the great religious and ethical systems. In brief, during the last few decades the discussed Sensate theories and practices have utterly degenerated and have led mankind to an extreme degree of ideological and practical demoralization—publicly approved by the governments and supported by a large portion of the Western and Soviet blocs of nations.

Fortunately for all of us, during the same recent decades of disintegration of the discussed Sensate ideologies and practices, new—and quite different—theories and practices have emerged and have slowly grown in this field. The new theories have convincingly shown that the factor of mutual aid, cooperation, and unselfish love has been at least as important a factor of biological evolution as the struggle for existence; that the role of mutual aid and friendly cooperation has been incomparably greater in human progress than the role of inimical rivalry, and violent coercion.[4] These new theories have shown further that, in his sound and creative behavior, man is determined by sympathy, benevolence, and unselfish love as much as by egotistic motives, hate, and sadistic impulses; and that the energy of this love is indispensable for generation, continuity, and growth of living forms, for survival and multiplication of the species, and particularly for survival and physical health of infants, and for their growth into mentally and morally sound citizens. The recent studies disclosed also that altruistic persons live longer than egotistic ones, that love is a powerful antidote against criminal, morbid and suicidal tendencies; against hate, fear, and psychoneuroses; that it performs important cognitive and aesthetic functions; is the loftiest, effective educational force for enlightenment and moral ennoblement of humanity; that it is the heart of a true freedom; that it can stop interindividual and intergroup conflicts, and can turn inimical relationships into amicable ones. Finally, that the minimum of unselfish love is absolutely necessary for the durable existence of any society, and that at the present catas-

trophic moment of human history an increased altruization of individuals and groups and extension of
unselfish love of everyone for everyone is a necessary
condition for the prevention of new wars and for
liberation of mankind from its gravest ills: bloody
conflicts, crime, insanity, and misery.[5]

From this outline of the new theories in this field
one can see again that these theories are in complete
agreement with the religious verity that Love is God
and God is Love and with the moral precepts of the
great religions.

It has been shown elsewhere that drastic re-
vision of many other basic theories of psychosocial
sciences have taken place for the last few decades:
in the problems of methods of social research, of
causality, of sociocultural structure and dynamics, of
the total character of explanation and interpretation
of politics and economics, ethics and law, fine arts
and other cultural values.[6] It is enough to say that
in all these problems the discussed struggle between
the decadent varieties of Sensate and the newly
merging Integral theories relentlessly goes on.

This struggle proceeds also in other compartments of today's culture and social life. In the *field
of philosophy* this double process has manifested
itself in increasing sterility and decline of recent materialistic, mechanistic, positivistic, and other Sensate
philosophies; and in emergence and growth of the
Phenomenological, the Existential, the Intuitive, the
Integral, the neo-Mystical, the neo-Thomist, the
neo-Vedantist, the neo-Taoist, and other philosophies congenial to the new Integral theories of the
total reality, cognition, human personality, and so on.

In *the realm of religion* during the last few decades, this struggle has shown itself in the simultaneous growth of: 1, a) militant atheism and b) modest religious revival; 2, a) in increased abuse and hypocritical misuse of Christianity and other great religions by the ruling groups, vested interests, and ignorant fanatics; and b) in spiritual purification and moral ennoblement of great traditional religions; 3, in emergence of: a) the ignorant and hate-laden pseudo-religious sects, and b) of the new, intensely spiritual and truly altruistic religious movements.

In *the ethical life of mankind* the double process has manifested itself, on the one hand, in extraordinary increase of wars and bloody revolutions that made this century the bloodiest out of twenty-five centuries identified with Greco-Roman and Western history; in utter bestiality shown in these wars and bloody conflicts; in increasing criminality, and other phenomena of extreme demoralization. On the other hand, the same recent period has displayed growth of moral heroism, sublime altruism, and organized movements for abolition of war, bloody strife, misery, exploitation, and injustice in their grossest forms.

The *fine arts* give witness, on the one hand to an utter vulgarization and uglification of decaying Sensate forms of music, literature, painting, sculpture, movies, television, and drama; growth of their negativism and pathological bent; the pseudo-art corrupting the beautiful, debunking all values, and centering around criminal's hideout, sex, insanity, and violence.[7] On the other hand, we have witnessed: emergence of the modern art as a revolt against this vulgar-pathological, Sensate art; and the first attempts at creation of new Integral forms of fine arts, meaningful in their content, beautifying the ugly, ennobling the ignoble — an inspiring and beautiful art, uplifting and enlightening us mentally, morally, and socially.

Among other things, this brief analysis shows that *the new rising socio-cultural order promises to give a spontaneous unification of religion, philosophy, science, ethics, and fine arts into one integrated system of supreme values of Truth, Goodness, and Beauty.* Such a unification signifies the end of conflicts of science, religion, fine arts and ethics with each other.

This struggle between the forces of the previously creative, now largely outworn Sensate order, and the emerging creative forces of a new — Integral — order is proceeding relentlessly in all fields of social and cultural life, and in the inner life of every one of us. The final outcome of this epochal struggle will greatly depend upon whether mankind can avoid a new world war. If this Apocalyptic catastrophe can be avoided, then the emerging creative forces will usher humanity into a new and magnificent era of its history.

CHAPTER IX

DECLINE OF SENSATE VALUES,
INSTITUTIONS AND IDEOLOGIES

The discussed double process of decay of Sensate and emergence of Integral institutions and cultural values is going on also in the field of political, economic, and social life. The decay of the Sensate political and social order proceeds both through: a) degeneration of its free, contractual institutions, values and ideologies into compulsory and fraudulent monsters born of the contractual parents; and b) an increasing depreciation and obsolescence of these parental institutions, values, and ideologies.

In order to grasp the full meaning of these statements, one must keep in mind that all the diverse forms of human relationship easily fall into three main classes: 1, *familistic,* permeated by mutual love, devotion, and sacrifice; 2, *free contractual* agreements of the parties for their mutual advantage, devoid of love, hate or coercion, but profitable for all contracting parties; and 3, *compulsory* relationships imposed by one party upon the others, contrary to their wishes and interests. Of these three relationships the familistic is the noblest, the compulsory is the worst, while the contractual occupies the intermediary position.

The proportion of each of these relationships in the total network of social relationships in each society varies from group to group and from period to period.[1] For instance, the total texture of social relationships of European mediaeval society from the

eighth to the twelfth century was mainly familistic,
in lesser degree compulsory, and only slightly contractual. From the sixteenth to the middle of the
eighteenth century the proportion of compulsory relationships notably increased.

1. Contractual Agreements and Politics

In the nineteenth century the total texture of
human relationships of Western societies became
predominantly contractual. This period was the
golden age of Western contractualism. During this
period Western society built a comfortable Sensate
house based upon contract, free agreement for
mutual advantage of its members, the citizens and
their government, employers and their employees,
and the members of other associations of free men.
Western society in that century became indeed a
fairly well-ordered contractual house inhabited by
almost free men governed by roughly free agreement. Its dominant capitalist system of economy
was a contractual system of economic relationship
between the parties involved, employers and employees. This contractual-capitalist economy was
quite different from the coercive system of slavery
and serfdom as well as from the system of relationships governing the members of a good family unified together into one "we" by mutual love, devotion,
and sacrifice. In difference from these, the capitalist system was based upon free contract between
employer and employees for mutual advantage. In
such an economy each person was almost a free
agent, freely choosing his occupation, freely accepting (or refusing) contractural agreements with his

employer or employees. Capitalism increased the efficiency of labor and machines, stimulated the increase of technological inventions, and led to a basic improvement in the material standard of living of the Western world.

In the political field the rise of contractual relations in the nineteenth century resulted in the elimination of autocratic, coercive governments and in their replacement by democratic political regimes, with the government contractually elected, contractually limited in its power, and bound to respect the inalienable rights of the citizen — his life, property, and pursuit of happiness, his liberties of speech, press, religion, association, choice of occupation, etc. The elective principle became the means of recruiting rulers and public officials. Contractual government of the people, for the people, and by the people largely replaced the autocratic governments by violence or through the wills of the rulers themselves.

Besides economic and political institutions, other important organizations became contractual. Liberty of religion transformed the previous, largely coercive, religious organizations into free contractual bodies of which one was free to become, or not to become, a member. A similar transformation occurred within the *family*. Marriage was declared a purely civil contract between the free parties, in contradistinction to compulsory marriage in which the parties were chosen, often against their wishes, by parents or other authorities. Becoming contractual in its establishment, marriage was made also contractual in its continuity and dissolution, in contrast to the mediaeval marriage which was indissoluble in principle; in exceptional cases it admitted only "separation from bed and board" *(divortium a mensa et thoro)*, and not a real divorce and termination of the marriage. Contractual liberties and inalienable rights of every person greatly expanded and permeated practically all organizations, up to even a contractual army of free volunteers in some Western countries.

In the nineteenth century Western man brought to fruition the fight for Sensate freedom, inalienable rights, and contractual order — begun at the end of the twelfth century. The first fruit of this fight was the Magna Charta of 1215, and during subsequent centuries the struggle continued in the form of revolutionary, reformatory, and other movements, until in the nineteenth century it resulted in a fairly successful realization of a free society of free men.

2. DISINTEGRATION OF CONTRACTUAL POLITICS

For several important reasons not to be discussed here,[2] the whole Sensate sociocultural order began to disintegrate at the beginning of the twentieth century; with its decay the contractual fabric of Western society became less and less free, and more compulsory in its political, economic, and social institutions. After 1914, in many Euro-American nations the contractual forms of government and capitalist economy almost ceased to exist, while in many others they have been increasingly distorted by the intrusion of coercive or fraudulent simulacra. Their place has been taken by various totalitarian forms of government and economy: Communist, Fascist, Nazi, Military, Pseudo-Socialist, Pseudo-

Democratic, and other varieties of Caesarism, Militarism, and Dictatorship.

In the contractual society of the nineteenth century, governments were elective and controlled only a small fraction of social relations and behavior of their citizens; even in this controlled area, the activities of governments were definitely limited by the constitutions, bills of rights, and laws of each nation. Beginning with the economic relations of production, distribution, and consumption, and ending with the choice of occupations, amusements, residence, marriage, religion, education, political affiliation, ideological preferences, and so on, all these matters were freely decided by the citizens and private groups.

In the completely or partially totalitarian nations of today the governments are self-appointed, not elected or contractual. If some of them still coerce their subjects to participate in so-called elections, these "elections" are but fraudulent mockery of free elections. And it is not individuals or private groups, but the government which now decides, controls, and regulates almost all behavior of citizens. In practically all the nations of the Communist bloc, plus such countries as Turkey, Saudi Arabia, Formosa, Iran, Pakistan, Southern Korea, Thailand, and others, regimentation and control are well-nigh complete; the government decides practically everything and the citizen nothing, except the choice between obeying unconditionally the orders of the government and going to prison, losing his property and perhaps his life. In so-called democratic and free countries, plus nations like Spain, Portugal, several countries of the Middle East and Latin America, the governmental regimentation is more restricted, but it has grown far beyond its limits in the nineteenth century and is still expanding. A disguised machinatory-compulsory oligarchic regime takes the place of the contractual regime of the nineteenth century. The formerly free citizen now finds himself an object of government experimentation. Not only is his conduct in economic, political, and other fields controlled, but even his mind and his thoughts are molded after patterns prescribed by the rulers. Compulsory regimes of self-appointed dictators and oligarchic cliques have largely replaced government of the people by the people and for the people. The free enterprise of capitalist economy is totally or largely supplanted by governmentally managed Communist, Fascist, Socialist, Planned, Welfare-State, and war regimented economies.

Such, in brief, is degeneration of the free contractual-political, economic, and social regimes of the West.

3. The Passing of Democratic Values

Similar degeneration has also occurred with many "democratic" values, procedures, and organizations. Free universal suffrage in the election of governments and in decisions of vital national problems has been either completely abolished or greatly restricted, or replaced by its fraudulent simulacra. Its place has been taken by either violent seizure of power by revolutionaries, militarists, and various juntas, or by economic pressures, demagogic machinations, and monopolistic propaganda through plutocratically or oligarchially controlled press, radio, television, and other means of communication. Naked force, assisted by fraud, has become the main method for establishment and functioning of many existing governments and power groups.

Similar decay through increasing emptiness and obsolescence has fallen also upon the principle of universal suffrage as the method of election of government in the contractual society. When governments elected by universal, direct, and secret ballot replaced governments by the "grace of God," or violent seizure of power, or oligarchic machinations, the principle of election was a great value and the best method of selection of the rulers and political leaders. It was especially fruitful in the comparatively small states and communities where most of the citizens well knew the competing candidates. When subsequently these communities grew into vast empires, when the whole electoral machinery became monopolized by small cliques of politicians, when these politicians began to decide who in each party was to be nominated for what position, when direct, personal knowledge of the candidates became impossible for 99 per cent of the voters, when political propaganda through press, radio, television, and other means of communication became monopolized by small caucuses of professional politicians and power groups; finally, when bribery, fraud, threats, punishments and murder began to be used as the instrumentalities of elective campaigns — then the value of the elective principle had largely evaporated. If in its true functions it has given "the government of the people, by the people, and for the people," it gives in its present hollow form only "government of politicians, by politicians, and for politicians." No wonder, therefore, that in lieu of considering voting as a great privilege, so regarded by the citizens of the true contractual society, voting is now regarded a waste of time by a large part of the voters. They prefer not to bother themselves with this nuisance and do not even vote in elections for chiefs of state. Depreciation of the value of voting has gone so far that in a number of the states citizens are coerced to vote under penalty of law! This fact alone testifies the enormous degradation of the elective principle; from the rank of a great privilege it has fallen to that of a burden imposed upon the citizens.

In other organizations, like the family, degeneration has assumed the form of weakening its unity, stability, and sanctity. The trends of ever-increasing divorce, desertion, pre-marital and extra-marital sex relations, childless marriages, growing infidelity and disloyalty, of decreasing mutual love, devotion, and responsibility of husband and wife, parent and child, are the undisputable manifestation of this degeneration.[3]

Free contractual labor unions have progressively turned either into compulsory government unions, or into semi-coercive political machines and labor-racketeering gangs, autocratically manipulated by corrupt politicians and racketeers, imposing their power by fraud, threat, and violence upon a vast proportion of laborers. A similar fate has overtaken other free associations: scientific, educational, artistic, recreational, and others. Directly or indirectly, the long arm of the totalitarian, oligarchic, and plutocratic ruling groups has also reached these organizations and is increasingly crushing their freedom, and regimenting their creative activities.

Finally, contractualism has degenerated shockingly in international relations. The triumph of contractualism in the nineteenth century led to agreements between governments, development of international law, and international arbitration courts like the Hague tribunal. These institutions helped prevent the explosions of wars and made the period from 1814 to 1914 one of the most peaceful centuries of Greco-Roman and Western history. In 1914 this peaceful order was abruptly terminated by the First World War. Beginning with 1914, the binding power of international treatises and contracts became weakened and international law was cast to the wind; all governments, without any exception whatsoever, turned to violence and fraud as the supreme arbiters of all international and national conflicts. The resulting wars and revolutions have made the twentieth century the bloodiest and most turbulent period of all the twenty-five recorded.[4] At the present time mankind is facing the danger of new Apocalyptic wars that threaten its very survival.

Thus "the proud citizen of the nineteenth century finds himself deprived of his security. His boasted individualism is trampled under foot: he is now an insignificant cog in a huge machine operated without regard to his wishes. His liberties and inalienable rights are largely gone. He has become a mere puppet. Millions of once proud citizens are shunted hither and thither, pushed and pulled about more unceremoniously than

slaves by their masters. They are drafted, de-
ported, imprisoned, tortured, and killed; or turned
into cannon fodder. Safety of life and security of
property are largely extinct."[5]

Few periods in human history have witnessed so
catastrophic a degeneration of their great social institutions and cultural values as we have had during
the first half of this century.

Increasing obsolescence of contractual relationships developed within Sensate society as a natural consequence of its essential properties. Under
conditions of ethical atomism, relativism, and potential nihilism of the Sensate system of values, together
with an ever-expanding desire for Sensate values of
wealth, bodily pleasures, material comfort, lust for
power, fame, and sex-freedom, the contractual relationships were bound to degenerate into pseudo-con-
tractual ones. In order for a contract to be a real
and free contract, four basic conditions must be
present: a) the contracting parties must have about
equal freedom to enter or not to enter the contract;
b) there must be an advantage from it for all the
contracting parties; c) after the conclusion of the
contract the parties must faithfully fulfill their obligations; d) though advantageous to the contracting
parties, the contract must not harm the vital interests of the society and persons not involved in the
contract.

With the aging of the Sensate order, the excessive relativism of its values, particularly its moral
atomism and cynicism, and its intensified struggles
for wealth, power and sensual pleasures, has made

neglect of these four conditions increasingly frequent. "Contractualism in such an atmosphere, tends by its very nature to degenerate into a lawless, normless, amoral, godless compulsion"[6] or pseudo-contract under duress. What is the use of the solemn declaration of equality of all men or even of equal rights of all citizens to "life, liberty, and the pursuit of happiness" when in actual social life we witness the gigantic inequality of the multimillionnaires and the hungry masses, human dust dominated by small and big bosses, beginning with a foreman or ward-politician and ending with the political, economic, and racketeering big shots? What is the cash-value of liberty of the press or other means of communication when the press, radio, and television are monopolistically controlled by a small group of the power elite? Such a monopoly makes all these liberties largely fictitious for all whose ideas threaten the vested interests of the oligarchic monopolists. Of what value is free choice of occupation when millions of the unemployed cannot find any job? Also useless are all the contracts broken by parties as soon as they become disadvantageous. Contracts between the members of criminal gangs, bosses of industry and finance, and members of a labor union are often profitable for these parties but detrimental to society as a whole. All such contracts, freedoms, and equalities become hollow, dead shells of the great values they once were. Patrick Henry's "Give me liberty or give me death" sounded true and inspiring in the conditions of its utterance. The same motto pompously repeated by a semi-crooked politician in his empty oration on the Fourth of July evokes only boredom and sarcastic irritation.

Similar degradation and obsolescence have been the fate of many ideologies of Sensate sociocultural order at its previous creative stage. Ideologies of John Locke, Rousseau, Marx, and other varieties of democratic, liberal, progressive, conservative, socialist, syndicalist, communist, anarchist ideologies; those of equality, freedom, free enterprise, planned economy, welfare society — all these ideologies which previously inspired are at present about dead. Their truths are exposed as errors, their fire is gone, and their ashes are cold. Remaining now are only their empty shells, clashed one against another by politicians in the incessant fight of one clique against another. As a result, *at the present time most of the nations, their political leaders and ideologists do not have any living, inspiring, and creative ideology which successfully meets the challenge of our time and wisely points a safe road to the grand future.* All they have instead is an atrocious concoction of odds and ends of obsolescent ideologies, mixed up with their "home-made" ideological crooning and jazz. If we are living in an age of confusion generally, this confusion is particularly great in the field of political ideologies and values.

The above outlines the trend of decline of Sensate political institutions, values, and ideologies. Let us now glance at a brighter trend of emergence of the seedlings of a new Integral sociopolitical order.

Chapter X

EMERGENCE OF A NEW ORDER

The contemporary decline of the Sensate Political Order is somewhat countered by the emergence of seedlings of a new, probably Integral sociopolitical system. The collapsing contractual house of Western man is now being replaced not only by the military barracks and vast concentration camps of totalitarian architects or by the Quonset huts, tourist cabins and cheap motels of the pseudo-democratic, oligarchic builders; here and there, in the vast human universe, there begin to appear the modest buildings of a new architectural style, nobler and better in its full development than even the contractual style of the nineteenth century. This new socio-political order aims to be built upon the up-to-date scientific knowledge and accumulated wisdom of humanity; it is animated not by the struggle for existence and rivalry of everybody against everyone, as the contractual, totalitarian, and oligarchic orders largely have been, but by the spirit of universal friendship, sympathy, and unselfish love with ensuing mutual aid of everyone to everybody.

So far there are only a few, comparatively modest, buildings of this new order; but if mankind can avoid the new suicidal wars and revolutions, these new buildings are bound to multiply rapidly and to develop into a magnificent familistic order of humanity.

Let us briefly survey these new beginnings.

1. Growth of Familistic Relationships and Organizations

First, while the contractual order of the West has been crumbling and has been replaced by the coercive totalitarian regime, many Asiatic and African societies have passed from the hitherto dominant coercive order to the more free, contractual system of social and political organization.

Such transition has been experienced by previously colonial peoples such as India, Indonesia, Pakistan, Tunis, and Morocco who regained political and social independence from their colonial masters. The total number of persons involved in this transition from the coercive to the roughly contractual and partly familistic order is hardly less than the total number of individuals involved in the transition from the contractual to the coercive order. In this way the regressive political change in the West is somewhat compensated for by the progressive political transformation of many Asiatic, African, and other societies.

Second, while the contractual order in international relations has largely crumbled, several new international institutions, such as the defunct League of Nations and the existing United Nations, have emerged and are trying to build a world-wide contractual order instead of the previous "parochial" agreements of a few governments with each other. Despite many a great defect, the United Nations and other international institutions of this kind contain great potentialities and can develop into important agencies of international peace, for the unification

of all the separate states into at least a loosely co-
ordinated world-community.

The third most important change consists in
the fact that not everything is coercive and fraudulent in the totalitarian and oligarchic regimes that
supplanted the contractual order; though the total
fabric of these regimes consists largely of the compulsory and fraudulent fibers, it contains also a considerable portion of familistic filaments. For instance, though the total network of social relationships of the Soviet political and economic system is
made up mainly of coercive fibers, it also contains a
considerable portion of familistic filaments and some
contractual fibrils. In contrast to Soviet Russia, the
total network of social relationships in the United
States and other so-called democratic nations consists mainly of the contractual, with the compulsory
and familistic filaments occupying a much smaller
place than they have in the Soviet system. This
means that the described degeneration of the contractual order of the nineteenth century into the
totalitarian and oligarchic has not been totally regressive; a part of the previous contractual relationships have been transformed into the much nobler
familistic relationships. These familistic relationships are "the hidden power" that gives to totalitarian systems their remarkable strength, moral prestige and partial justification. This tendency is also
responsible for the world-wide admiration and imitation of the Soviet social, economic, and political
system on the part of countless millions of previously
colonial peoples and of the down-trodden and
cheated masses in many contractual and oligarchic

systems. Without ennobling, unifying, and inspiring familistic relationships, the purely coercive part of the Soviet, the Chinese, and other coercive-familistic societies of our time would have fallen to pieces long ago, and would have had no chance for enormous expansion and diffusion of these systems in today's human universe. The familistic relations are exactly the powerful secret weapon of successful growth, particularly of the Communist and Socialist totalitarianisms of our time.

Side by side with inhuman regimentation and enslavement of millions of their citizens, the Soviet and similar regimes have liberated these millions from many forms of previous subjugation and exploitation; inspired them with the dignity of responsible members of the new society; alleviated the poverty and misery of vast down-trodden masses; opened to all capable citizens highways to the highest educational and social positions, stimulated the potential creativity of a large part of their population, energetically developed industrial and economic activities of their nations, and demonstrated stern but capable leadership during epochal sociocultural reconstructions. What is still more important, their policies of collectivization, nationalization, and partial equalization, have evoked in their citizens not only the behavior of regimented prisoners, but also the conduct of the free collective "we" spontaneously united into one vast family by mutual sympathy and responsibility.

Contrary to the prevalent opinion of the "democratic" ideologists, the populations of Soviet Russia and China are united into one energetic, creative, and courageous national "we," not so much by the painful cement of coercion as by the enduring familistic bonds in which the suffering or joy, creative achievement or failure of one member is fully shared by the others. In this type of community, as in a good family, the lesser interests of each individual are largely transcended by the greater interests of the whole community and everyone feels himself an indispensable partner of the whole, giving of his very best and receiving from the rest their best service and help. Such a community is something quite different from "the lonely crowds" of today's contractual and oligarchic societies, for in the familistic communities there are few, if any, strangers or lonely souls engrossed in selfish ambitions and lilliputian rivalries, few free isolated individuals who do not care for anybody and are not cared for by anyone. There is very little of the "it does not concern me," or "mind your own business."

"The strong mutual attachment of the members of the familistic society is not due to any contract or formal covenant or calculation of pleasure and pain, advantage and disadvantage. A devoted mother gladly passes many a sleepless night with her sick child, not because of an implicit or explicit contract between her and the child or between herself and society. Her action is the result of her spontaneous love for her child. Much the same is true of real friends. If one befriends another on the basis of a mere contract, or from motives of profit or pleasure, he is a pseudo-friend. A real friend, as Aristotle rightly observes, is 'one who . . . does what is good (or what he believes to be good) for another for that

other's sake, and one wishes his friend . . . to live for
that friend's own sake',[1] and not because the friend
gives him pleasure or is useful for him."[2]

2. THE MYSTERIOUS POWER OF LOVE

Still little known, the mysterious energy of this
true friendship or unselfish love is an incomparably
nobler and potentially greater factor in human behavior than the energy of the utilitarian factors
dominant in contractual interactions of human beings; it is especially great, compared with the energy
of rude force and fraud powering coercive relationships. In the form of mutual aid and cooperation,
this unifying benevolent energy has played at least
as important a role in the biological evolution of the
species as the dividing and selfish energy of the
struggle for existence.[3]

The rapidly increasing body of evidence in contemporary biology, psychology, sociology and other
branches of science shows that this energy of love is
indispensable to the generation, continuity, and
growth of living forms; for survival and multiplication of a species; and for maintenance of health and
integrity, especially of human individuals. Recent
studies show further that "creative love or true
friendship (a) can stop aggressive interindividual
and intergroup attacks; (b) can transform inimical
relationships into amicable ones; (c) that love begets
love, and hate generates hate; (d) that the energy
of love is a life-giving form, necessary for physical,
mental, and moral health; (e) that altruistic persons
live longer than egoistic individuals; (f) that children deprived of love tend to become morally and

socially defective; (g) that love is a powerful antidote against criminal, morbid, and suicidal tendencies, against fear, hate, and mental disorders; (h)
that love performs important cognitive and aesthetic
functions; (i) that it is the loftiest and most effective
educational force for enlightenment and moral ennoblement of humanity; (j) that it is the heart and
soul of freedom and of all main moral and religious
values; (k) that its minimum is absolutely necessary
for the durable existence of any society, and especially for a harmonious social order and creative
progress; (1) that love can pacify international conflicts; (m) that, finally, at the present catastrophic
moment of human history an increased 'production,
accumulation, and circulation' of love-energy, or a
notable altruization of persons and groups, institutions and culture, is a necessary condition for the
prevention of new wars and for the alleviation of
enormously increased interhuman strife."[4]

Exactly this energy of unselfish love in its rude
or sublime varieties animates, motivates, and powers
the familistic forms of human behavior, relationships, and social, political, and economic organizations. Being one of the three highest energies known
to man (the energies of Truth, Beauty, and Goodness or Unselfish-Creative Love) it ennobles all
familistic persons, communities or nations, inspires
them with great and constructive tasks, and blesses
them with the strength and creativity necessary for
realization of these high objectives.

This explains why a transformation of part of
the contractual relationships into the familistic ones
and the growth of the familistic elements among

totalitarian regimes and democratic and oligarchic societies is of epochal significance.

Fourth, familistic social institutions are proliferating not only in the totalitarian but also in the democratic nations in the forms of Welfare and Socialist States, Progressive Republicanism, and Liberal Democracy; in the growth of various familistic communities like the Society of Brothers, the Hutterite, the Mennonite, and the Friends' Communities, and in the ever-increasing social service, cooperation, and mutual aid on a local level. All rapidly growing familistic relationships, communities, brotherhoods, and sociocultural institutions are forerunners of this new Integral-sociocultural order. If fully developed, this order promises to be nobler and finer than the coercive and contractual orders of the past.

Let us now glance briefly at some of the changes which should be expected in the existing governments and political regimes if these institutions are going to become increasingly familistic and integral, based upon the available scientific knowledge and wisdom, animated by the spirit of unselfish love and free from ugliness in their aspirations and administrations.

3. DECLINE OF COERCIVE RELATIONSHIPS

A growth of Familistic social and political regimes implies a progressive decrease of compulsory relations in all interhuman interactions and organizations. This decrease tends to be quantitative and qualitative: the proportion of coercive fibers, as well as their coarseness in the social texture of all states and their governments, is bound to decrease steadily. This means a quantitative and qualitative decline of totalitarian and coercive governments in all kinds of social organizations. The discussed universal disarmament will largely contribute to this trend; if all governments are deprived of armed forces they cannot practice the coercive measures as liberally as when they have vast armies at their disposal, as coercive agents. Controlling only a small police force, the future governments must develop more refined and ingenious means for a fruitful discharge of their duties, maintenance of harmonious social order and promotion of their citizens' well-being.

The decrease in coercive relationships does not mean their complete disappearance from the human universe. It is improbable that all human beings can be transformed into rational, morally perfect creatures. Even with a notable decrease, a considerable fund of selfish ambitions and rivalry, irrational passions and hate, stupidity and conflict will still be operating in the human world. This will make unavoidable some amount of coercive control in relationships of governments and governed, and in relationships of citizens with one another. This survival of coercive, antagonistic, and hateful forces in the coming familistic order does not exclude, however, a substantial decrease of these forces in humanity. Any tangible decrease of their operations means a notable moral and social improvement of mankind and the man-made universe.

4. Re-direction of the Forces of Strife

A further notable decrease of the disastrous

effects of these forces of interhuman strife, hatred, coercion, and mistreatment can be achieved by re-channeling their outbursts and re-directing their aggressive energy. In the struggle for existence, irrational passions and hateful emotions manifest themselves and find their satisfaction almost ex-clusively in generating and fueling all forms of inter-human strife beginning with cut-throat competition, inhuman coercion, and merciless exploitation, and ending with murderous wars, bloody revolts and crime. Their energy can, however, be re-directed in such a way that instead of serving destructive tasks it can be turned to constructive purposes. Re-chan-neling of the energy of hatred can give an example of this re-direction.

Hatred is still one of the most powerful emotions of man and one of the most efficient "motors" of human behavior. In an overwhelming majority of human beings it cannot be quickly eliminated or even greatly weakened. It can, however, be re-channeled for serving different "works" and "operations." Hitherto it has "powered" mainly interindividual and intergroup conflicts. Instead of this function, its power can be used for exten-sion of love and for binding mankind into one solidary body. How? *By redirecting the power of hatred from its present channels of interindividual and intertribal conflicts into a new "pipe line" serving the sacred war of humanity against the most terrible, most implacable, eternal, and com-mon enemies of every human being, every group, and of the whole of mankind: against death, physical and mental disease, gravest criminality, stupidity, ignorance, interhuman strife, ugliness, poverty, fruitless suffering, nature's calamities, in-terhuman hatred itself, and a host of other forces inimical to every man's creative growth and everybody's vital, mental, and moral well-being.*

Instead of setting man against man, and group against group, the power of hatred can be directed against these eternal and universal enemies of humanity. They are so formidable that the whole reservoir of mankind's hatred can easily be spent in this fight. Their merciless pressure is so enormous that everybody's fighting impulses can find the fullest satisfaction in this sacred war. With a minimum of teaching, preaching, and propaganda, everybody's patriotic ethos and pathos in this sacred war can be easily incited, maintained and exalted to the highest pitch of intensity ever reached in any tribal war. If Hitler as the common enemy could temporarily bind together Stalin, Roosevelt, and Churchill; if the Kremlin Communist government, as the common enemy, could unify into one military alliance the most heterogeneous governments of the Western bloc; still more easily can mankind be unified into one permanent solidary body by its perennial common enemies.

To sum up: if a fraction of the resources spent for inciting tribal wars is used for arousing the holy war of humanity against its nonhuman adversaries, the most powerful — intellectual, emotional, and volitional — unification of the whole of mankind for such a war can be accomplished. In this way the elemental power of hatred will be destroying interhuman hatred, the aggressive propensities of man will be fighting interhuman aggressions, and the "fighting instincts" of man will be serving the task of the unification of humanity freed from interhuman wars.[5]

By similar re-channeling, the forces of predatory competition and the struggle for existence can also serve to pacify and harmonize the social life of mankind, instead of intensifying interhuman conflicts. Competition in humility and unselfish service, the only competition approved by the great monastic orders and competition in the exploration and use of outer space for the benefit of mankind can serve as examples of this re-direction. Through this sort of re-channeling, the remaining coercive relationships within states and other organizations can be reduced to a still smaller minimum.

This can be further cut through replacement of compulsory fibers by re-established contractual filaments.

5. PARTIAL RENAISSANCE OF CONTRACTUAL RELATIONSHIPS

If in the decaying Sensate order no substantial revival of true contractual relationships is possible, a notable renaissance of such relationships can be expected in the emerging Integral and Familistic sociocultural order. Among other things, the new Integral order implies replacement of the excessive relativism of the dying Sensate culture by universal moral values accepted by and binding upon all. Establishment of such a moral order serves as a solid foundation for the restoration of genuine contractual relationships — binding, freely entered, and advantageous for all. Many of today's coercive relationships are likely to become contractual ones. Many an arbitrary and dictatorial function of the existing rulers is bound to be limited again by new Bills of Rights, Constitutions, and laws. At the same time these safeguards will help the governments in the proper discharge of their duties and functions.

To sum up: *the total network of social relationships in the emerging state and other organizations will increasingly consist of familistic fibers, then contractual ones, with an ever decreasing portion of compulsory relationships and their by-products: wars, violent strifes, crimes, and maltreatment of man by man.* Only this kind of social organization can save mankind from catastrophic termination of its creative life. In spite of the enormous propaganda of the partisans of totalitarian and contractual (democratic and oligarchic) regimes, their efforts to revive and to maintain these regimes are bound to fail. These types of social organizations have become largely obsolescent and disserviceable at the present stage of human history. Only the predominantly familistic type of society can successfully meet the tremendous challenge of our time.

The emerging Integral and Familistic sociocultural order implies several radical changes in the governments of the states, big business corporations, labor unions, and other powerful organizations. Let us cogitate a little as to what some of these changes are likely to be.

Chapter XI

TOWARDS GOVERNMENT OF
SCIENTISTS, SAGES AND SAINTS

Of many forthcoming changes three significant trends in the qualifications of the new governments are already observable. First, a growing requirement for higher intelligence, wisdom, and knowledge among the top-rulers of the governments; second, an increasing requirement for supreme moral integrity, almost saintliness, in the ranks of the governing elite; third a developing pressure for replacement of their tribal standpoint by the universal standpoint of mankind as a whole.

1. The Increasing Power of Science in Governments

The first of these trends manifests itself in the rapidly increasing role of scientists and experts in planning, developing, controlling, and executing an ever-increasing part of important governing activities and policies.

Many of the top rulers of existing governments, corporations, and labor unions are already largely figureheads rather than self-willed, energetic rulers. This is true even of such omnipotent ruling groups as the Soviet government and the Politbureau, the government of the United States and the Pentagon elite. To the superficial observer they appear to be forceful rulers determining the course of history by their deliberate decisions. A deeper investigation shows a notable part of their policies and actions to be merely the execution of the silent orders of recent scientific discoveries and inventions. These discoveries and inventions have made obsolescent most of what these top rulers learned two or three decades ago in preparing for their ruling activities, as well as their plans of even a few years ago. The top rulers are therefore executing policies which they do not themselves understand. Their present preoccupation with nuclear weapons, missiles, sputniks, and with still more modern scientific inventions is a typical illustration of the above statements. In their school and early professional work none of the statesmen and politicians received training for such military, diplomatic, and political activities. Before 1940 neither the Truman nor the Stalin administration, neither Eisenhower nor Khrushchev, neither the supreme commanders, generals, and admirals, nor any of today's leading statesmen and politicians had the fuzziest vision of the atomic, hydrogenic, and outer-space policies which contemporary top rulers are now carrying on. Each of the recent important scientific advances has forced them to fundamentally revise their plans and replace them with new and quite different diplomatic, military, economic, educational, and other policies. In this sense, today's ruling statesmen and politicians are increasingly becoming mere figurehead-executors of the silent orders of science and technology.

These "orders" are usually conveyed to them by their scientific experts, advisers, and committees. The top-rulers of practically all existing governments have a number of scientific committees specially appointed to advise the rulers in their main policies. Without the preliminary advice of a respectable scientific committee the rulers rarely venture to initiate any important policy. Though the recommendations of these scientific committees are supposedly merely advisory, in reality they are much more regularly followed by the rulers than many an obligatory decision of the statesmen and politicians themselves. Despite its free and advisory nature, any scientific truth is more compelling and authoritative than any command of the most autocratic ruler. For this reason, the recommendations of the more exact physical and biological advisory committees are followed by the rulers more regularly than those of experts in the less precise social and humanistic sciences. All in all, a large part of the governing activities of contemporary rulers already represents a mere implementation of the orders of science and technology, and there is reason to believe that this trend will increase rapidly until it embraces almost all policies and activities of the governments.

Such a trend portends the eventual withering of the hitherto existing "governments of politicians, by politicians, and for politicians" and their replacement by "governments of scientists and experts." The politician-ruler is increasingly becoming a sort of puppet or robot, and there is no advantage in main-execute the demands of science better than the non-scientific, largely ignorant, politician-rulers. Most of the present statesmen and politicians are persons who have not had advanced scientific training in any field of science except, perhaps, a training in the applied art of law and a superficial training in the semi-scientific disciplines of economics and politics. Many of them know little about even the applied art of law and sociological, psychological, economic, and political theories. In the past, when science and technology were little developed, the governments of politicians were the only available governments. At the present time, the enormous advances of the natural sciences and the more modest maturing of the social and humanistic disciplines have rendered useless the ruler-politicians who should know everything, but actually know very little. When any government or political regime becomes so antiquated, its days of life are numbered; it is destined to fall into oblivion in a comparatively short time. History is already writing a thrilling drama, *Death of a Politician*, similar to the well-known play *Death of a Salesman*. This trend is pregnant with many changes in the structure, personnel, and functions of the ruling elites of the states, the corporations, the labor unions, and other powerful organizations. For instance, the trend is likely to call forth basic changes in the constitutional laws defining hereditary rule, election, and self-appointment of the rulers. Instead of property-race-nationality-religion-domicile and the other traditional qualifications for voting, being elected or appointed, or becoming heir to any ruling position, the new laws are likely to require from the voters and the candidates an adequate and ever-greater scientific knowledge in the field of their sought-after governing activity. It is likely also that for election to many high offices, universal suffrage will be replaced either by appointment or voting of a limited body of scientific experts. The increased requirements for scientific qualifications may eventually exclude from inheritance of a throne or other top-ruling position all heirs who are scientifically incompetent, even though they may be otherwise entitled to inherit such a position. As this trend grows, the structure, personnel, and functions of the governments will change radically. In a government of scientists the traditional statesmen-politicians will have little chance to play the important roles they play now. Charitably we may wish them the fullest possible enjoyment of their present governing positions as long as they may last. A few decades from now the governments of politicians, by politicians, and for politicians are likely to be as rare as white elephants. Their place will probably be taken by governments of and by scientists and experts. Whether such a government will also become the *oligarchic* government of scientists, by scientists, and *for* scientists is the question to be discussed now.

2. A GOVERNMENT OF SCIENTISTS?

Should such an oligarchic government "of, by, and for" scientists develop (as it did with the government of, by, and for politicians), such an oligarchy of scientists would hardly be durable, nor could it give to mankind the best possible regime. Nor could it insure us against unlimited wars or be the most capable builder of lasting peace and harmonious order.

In their empirical forms, science and technology are morally and socially neutral. Almost any scientific discovery or invention can be used for good or evil purposes. An airplane can be used for the bombing of a peaceful population or for a charity mission. Discoveries and harnessings of nuclear energy can be used for mass-extermination of human beings or for peaceful satisfaction of humanity's needs. Similarly, scientists as scientists have been serving, and continue to serve, good as well as evil purposes. After all, most of the destructive discoveries and inventions, beginning with the stone-age arms and ending with the modern nuclear bombs, poisonous gas, bacteriological means of warfare, bombers, missiles, etc., have been discovered and invented by professional or non-professional scientists and inventors. At all periods of human history there have always been official or unofficial scientists and inventors who have intentionally worked upon destructive, murderous, and anti-social discoveries — inventions made either for their own satisfaction, for the protection of their society, or to the order of various governments. Leonardo da Vinci, serving the evil purposes of Cesare Borgia at one period of his life, is a classic example of scientists of this kind. At the present time there is no scarcity of scientists and inventors available to governments or private corporations for inventing means of destruction. Many of them are quite inspired by, and absorbed in, this sort of work, and they try their best to achieve their deadly purposes. If anything, this sort of scientist has probably always outnumbered those who refuse to do scientific research for destructive and evil goals. Fortunately for us, we also have constructive scientists and inventors. Although their number seems to be growing, they still comprise the minority of socially responsible seekers of truth, compared with the morally irresponsible misusers of science.

The moral neutrality of science and scientists is also shown by the *lack of close causal or statistical connection between morality (or criminality) and scientific (school) education and intelligence; and by the lack of causal or probabilistic ties between the movement of scientific discoveries and inventions on the one hand, and wars, bloody revolutions, and crimes on the other.* At the present time we have more than 163,000 cases investigated from the standpoint of whether there is close connection between intelligence, amount of schooling (or scientific education), and criminality. All these studies indicate that there seems to be no close relationship between these phenomena. Statistically expressed, "the coefficients of colligation between delinquency and illiteracy fluctuate in various studies from minus .09 to plus .24; between delinquency and amount of schooling, from minus .12 to plus .19; between criminality and school progress, from .46 to .52; between delinquency and educational achievement about minus .46. Considering that the coefficient of colligation is a still less reliable symptom of causal relationship than the coefficient of correlation, the foregoing coefficients of colligation indicate a lack of close relationship between intelligence and delinquency.[1]

This explains why among the monarchs and the chiefs of states the politically great and mentally bright rulers are no better morally than the politically poor and mentally dull rulers. If anything, the brighter and greater rulers tend to be slightly more amoral and criminal than the poor chiefs of states. The same can be observed among the highest ranks of military rulers and executives of big corporations, labor unions, and other organizations.

That scientific and technological progress does not decrease wars and bloody revolutions or their destructiveness can be seen from the following confrontation of the movement of scientific discoveries and inventions, and the number of universities on the one hand and the movement of wars and revolutions on the other from the twelfth to the twentieth century.[2]

Centuries	Index of Magnitude of War (Measured by War-Casualty per 1 million of European population)	Index of Magnitude of Revolutions in Europe	Number of Universities, Colleges and Technical Institutes in the Western World	Number of Scientific Inventions, Discoveries per Century
XII	2 to 2.0	763	5	12
XIII	3 to 5.0	882	18	53
XIV	6 to 9.0	827	30	65
XV	8 to 11.0	748	57	127
XVI	14 to 16.0	509	98	429
XVII	45	605	129	691
XVIII	40	415	180	1574
XIX	17	766	603	8527
XX	52*	295	753	862†

* 1900-1925 only
† 1900-1908 only

Moreover, with the increase in education, scientific discoveries, and inventions from the twelfth to the twentieth century, crime has not decreased; if anything, in the recent decades, at least, it has tended to increase. Furthermore, statistical data show that comparatively illiterate persons, nations, and groups are not more criminal than the literate, scientifically and technically advanced persons, nations, and groups. The intellectual elite of the past few centuries, distinguished for their scientific genius and creativity, have hardly been morally superior to the less brilliant rank and file. We live in the most scientific, most technological, and most intellectually educated century; and it is this same century which is the bloodiest, most turbulent, most inhuman, and possibly most criminal of all the preceding twenty-five centuries of Greco-Roman and Western history, so far as wars, revolutions, and crimes are concerned.

These considerations and their evidence show why the governments of scientists and experts are not necessarily more moral and less criminal than the governments of politicians. Therefore, the government of scientists is hardly a better guarantee against world war and bloody civil strife than the hitherto existing governments of the politicians of wealth, military might, oligarchic big business, and elective machinations, or the hereditary governments by the grace of God, brute force, or good luck. The governments of, by, and for scientists can easily fail in the attempt to solve the gigantic tasks of our transitory period. The knowledge of each of the scientific administrators is altogether too narrow and too specialized. It needs to be supplemented by a much broader wisdom that can integrate a multitude of specialized skills into one unified system aimed at realization of the best possible form of human society on this planet. Side by side with scientists the good government of the nearest future needs to have at least a few sages to perform successfully this task of integration of the narrow knowledge of each of the scientific administrators.

3. NEED FOR UNIVERSAL MORAL PRINCIPLES

The discussed amorality of science and scientific experts needs to be guided by universal and perennial moral principles in order to serve only the good and not the evil purposes. Without such guidance the government of scientific experts may turn out to be even more disastrous than that of politicians. These universal and eternal moral imperatives are sublimely formulated in the *Sermon on The Mount,* and in the essentially similar moral commandments of all great religions and ethical systems. Many view these precepts as manifestations of a natural law, divine law, or eternal law. These principles are also incorporated in practically all known criminal codes (beginning with the earliest codes such as the *Laws of Hammurabi* or the Ancient Egyptian law-norms, and ending with the latest criminal codes enacted in our time) and are enunciated by the moral and legal taboos of practically all known preliterate groups as well. Contrary to the prevalent belief in the unlimited relativity of moral and legal precepts, a more serious investigation of these phenomena shows that, side by side with the secondary, local, and ever-changing precepts and rules, all the great religious and secular ethical systems, criminal codes, moral taboos and obligatory mores of primitive peoples, all conceptions of the natural law, have a set of universal, perennial, unchangeable moral and legal norms of conduct, like the familiar Judaeo-Christian Ten Commandments. The only change-

able element of these eternal principles has been the
size of the in-groups to whose members these imperatives are to be applied and in which they are en-
forced. Thus, the commandment: "Thou shalt not
kill," found in all moral and legal codes, taboos and
mores of all societies of all periods, is a universal and
eternal principle. In the terms of the old Roman
law, it is *quod natura omnia animalia docuit;* in
Cicero's sense it is *aeternum quiddam quod univer-
sum mundum regeret imperandi prohibendique
sapientia.* But in almost all the past and even in the
present societies it has been applied only to the members of one's own in-group, be it preliterate clan,
tribe, family, community, city, nation, or religious-
racial-ethnic-political-economic-occupational group.
Up to the present time the obligatory application
and enforcement of this commandment has not been
extended beyond one's own tribe over the whole of
mankind. The principle thus remains universally
valid for all who want to follow the true moral principle, just as the proposition "two plus two make
four" is a universal and perennial verity in mathe-
matics. What has been changeable about both of
these propositions is not the principles themselves,
but the external circumstances of their applications.
Not all human beings have known them; some individuals and groups misunderstood and miscalcu-
lated them; some others intentionally transgressed
them; and most human beings and groups applied
them only to a very limited human tribe or a limited
set of material objects.

The same can be said of other *basic* moral imperatives and legal precepts;[3] they are universal,
eternal, and unchangeable for all who want to follow

valid moral principles just as the *basic* laws of logical
and mathematical thought and the basic principles
of science are universal and perennial for all who
want to think correctly and have valid knowledge of
scientific phenomena. The secondary propositions
and rules of both — moral and scientific — systems
are temporal, parochial, and everchanging. Furthermore, there have always been people who are ignorant of many ethical and scientific verities; there
have always been intentional or unintentional trans-
gressors of moral verities and scientific truths. But
all these changeable elements in moral and scientific
propositions and the phenomena and values they
deal with do not eliminate their universal and
eternal validity.

At the present stage of human history, universal
literacy and knowledge of the basic principles of
science are becoming necessary for all human beings.
Through obligatory education in elementary and
high schools, literacy and elementary knowledge of
science have progressively spread over almost the
whole world. This basic knowledge is now required
not only of an aristocratic minority, but of all, and
the actual spread of such a knowledge has largely
passed from the limited, tribal stage to the universal
stage of mankind.

Similar transition from a parochial to a universal moral standpoint has been occurring in human
history. The passage from tribal knowledge and
practice of moral verities to universal knowledge and
the practice of these verities has been taking place in
the human universe, especially in the last few centuries. During this time the development of transportation and communication has made mankind in-

creasingly interdependent. For the first time in human history, the term "mankind" now is beginning to mean something more than the mere sum of human individuals. It now denotes a different reality, namely a unified and tangibly interdependent body in which all parts of human population are dependent upon the whole species and the species is dependent upon its parts. In other words, mankind has largely passed from a multitude of causally independent groups often entirely isolated from each other, frequently knowing nothing of each other, to the stage of one unified, universal interdependent whole.

In this universalist stage of an interdependent humanity, the tribal moral standpoint: my country right or wrong, has become even more obsolescent than the tribal standpoint in knowledge and application of the basic scientific principles; it has ceased to serve the useful purposes which it served when mankind was not united in one interdependent body. At the present time, any aggrandizement of one's in-group at the cost of other outer-groups is like an attempt to cure one part of our body at the expense of others. Since mankind now is a tangibly unified, interdependent body, the attempt to improve (economically or politically) our own in-groups by harming other parts of mankind leads invariably to harmful results for the whole human race, as well as for our own in-group. The same is true for other universal, perennial moral precepts. If and when they are applied by any group on a tribal scale, the harmful results of such an obsolescent application usually boomerang upon the aggressive group itself, inflicting harm upon mankind as a whole as well.

Recent decades have given an abundant body of proofs for these conclusions. No matter which of the governments and nations initiated the First and the Second World Wars, none of the nations (especially none of the aggressive war-starting nations) has profited by these wars. In the long run all the pre-war nations have become the losers in these and the "brush-wars" of this century; all of them have had to pay for their violations of moral laws by needless losses of millions of human lives; by losses of the health and vitality of still more numerous millions; by disintegration of several of the great empires; by perdition of several pre-war governments, or by the violent overthrow, degradation, or annihilation of other pre-war ruling groups. These wars have caused limitless suffering in all nations; they have destroyed one-fifth of the inhabited territory of the earth, including its cities and villages; they have impoverished a vast portion of mankind; they have destroyed a large part of the natural resources and accumulated wealth in all the belligerent nations; finally, these wars have robbed all nations of their sense of security, moral integrity, human dignity, and creative hope in the future. At present, the sinister shadows of death and destruction hover over the whole human race. Even the few nations (like the United States) which for a short time seemed to have profited by the wars find themselves at the present time in a much graver situation than before the wars.

This Nemesis for the obsolescent tribal misuse of universal and eternal moral laws has been no less clearly manifested by the smaller "brush-wars" of the last two decades. None of the participant nations in either the Korean, the Indonesian, the Indo-Chinese, the Israel-Arab, the abortive English-Yemen, the French-Algerian, or in other "brush-wars" has really profited by these wars. Each of the belligerent nations has lost a great deal vitally, economically, mentally, morally, politically, as well as in terms of security, happiness, creativity, and moral dignity. The same Nemesis is strikingly visible in practically all violent tribal revolutions and revolts and racial, religious, economic, internal strife. In a short period the disastrous consequences of each of these internal strifes have boomeranged upon their initiators and all participants, and quickly turned today's victor into tomorrow's victim and yesterday's gainers into losers.

To sum up: just as the scientific training of a small aristocratic minority of the past has now been replaced by universal, obligatory training in basic science for everyone, so the tribal training in, and practical application of, basic moral principles is being replaced now by universal, obligatory training of everyone, and by practical application of these precepts by everyone to everyone. This replacement of the tribal moral standpoint by the universal is no longer a mere pious wish, but the most urgent necessity.

4. THE NEED FOR MORAL LEADERSHIP

The foregoing considerations explain why the ascending governments of scientists and experts need the efficacious guidance of universal and eternal moral imperatives.

This moral control of scientific governments can be achieved in several ways and through diverse moral agencies. Some of the scientists themselves (including scholars and philosophers) have always been persons of eminent moral integrity and leadership. At the present time, a notable portion of them is faithfully discharging both scientific and moral duties by following the universal and eternal moral precepts, and refusing to develop destructive weapons and arms, and protesting against war, internal strife, and the misuse of nuclear power for military purposes. They are among the groups leading the fight for a better realization of the basic moral values, and against great evils still operating in the human universe, including the evils of transgressing the eternal moral precepts and the evils of false dogmas and demoralizing ideologies. As members of governing bodies, leaders, and shapers of public opinion, morally responsible scientists, scholars, and philosophers can and do contribute to the moral guidance of governments and the public at large. The efficacy of their moral control may be notably increased by the scientific discovery of new effective methods of moral transformation of man and the man-made universe.[4]

The number of such scientists is now increasing, and when they compose an overwhelming majority in the scientific and scholastic professions, they are bound to become one of the greatest agencies for the moral ennoblement of mankind.

Besides morally responsible scientists, scholars, and philosophers, the discussed guidance and control of government can most effectively be performed by religious leaders and agencies, especially by the saintly heroes of spirituality and the sublime apostles of an unselfish, creative love. Religious leaders and agencies have always exercised spiritual guidance and moral control of governments and rulers. In the Ideational cultures the supremacy of spiritual over secular power is explicitly recognized and the theocratic governments of such societies are made up of religious leaders and agencies.[5] In Sensate and Integral cultures, the influence of the official religious hierarchy is lesser than in Ideational cultures, but it is still considerable. The influence of the apostles of love remains great in Integral and even in Sensate societies.

The oft-observed decline in the effectiveness of moral control of religious leaders over the governments and public at large is due mainly to their own moral and spiritual deterioration. Once they become the supreme spiritual and secular governments in Ideational cultures, theocratic rulers begin to suffer from the corruptive effects of their power and increasingly tend to transgress basic moral imperatives in their preachings and practices. In Sensate cultures, their materialistic and hedonistic values are largely responsible for a deterioration of moral and spiritual standards of their religious leaders. Instead of realization of the values of the kingdom of God, they begin to strive increasingly for the values of this world, power, wealth, material comfort, hedonistic pleasures, fame, popularity, etc. They tend to preach and practice tribal precepts quite different from (sometimes even opposite to) the everlasting moral imperatives. For instance, in such periods the leaders and agencies of Christian and other great religions fairly frequently substitute "Thou shalt kill" for "Thou shalt not kill." Similar distortion of other basic moral principles has occurred in practically all religious bodies which have grown into enormous and powerful empires, with their own hierarchies, rigid dogmas, and elaborate ritual. In their periods of moral lassitude and spiritual fatigue, religious leaders and agencies naturally exert much weaker moral guidance and control than in periods of their complete dedication to uncontaminated moral and spiritual values.

In recent times, such religious and moral leaders as Gandhi, Vinoba Bhave, L'Abbee Pierre, Albert Schweitzer, and a legion of unsung servants of Infinite, Pure, and Creative Love have possibly been the most influential force in the moral guidance of the governments and ennoblement of humanity. Their influence is not due to theological or ideological excellence, to a high position in religious hierarchy or in society, nor is it due to the writing of learned treatises in the field of ethics, or to scientific research in the physics of morals, statistics of mores, or psychoanalysis of a "schizophrenia of good-and-evil." Their influence seems to be coming directly from a superabundance of the supreme energy of unselfish love with which they are graced and which they indefatigably express in their thoughts, words, and deeds. Their influence comes from the same source which made Jesus, Buddha, and other apostles of Love possibly the most influential individuals among all the leaders in human history. "After all, Jesus, Buddha, Mahavira, Lao-Tzu, or Francis of Assisi had neither arms, nor physical force, nor wealth, nor any of the worldly means for exerting influence upon millions and for determining the historical destinies of nations and cultures. Nor to obtain their influence did they appeal to hate, envy, greed, and other selfish lusts of human beings. Even their physical organism was not that of the heavyweight champion. And yet, together with a handful of their followers, they reshaped the minds and behavior of untold millions, transformed cultures and social institutions, and decisively conditioned the course of history. None of the greatest conquerors and revolutionary leaders can even remotely compete with these apostles of love in the magnitude and durability of the change brought about by their activities."[6]

Anyone who happens to be selected and anointed by an abundant grace of the supreme, unselfish love continues to exert at the present an effective and constructive influence upon mankind such as these apostles of love have exerted in the past. In our time their moral guidance is more acceptable to many than that of the high officials of religious hierarchy because they do not try to grind any theological-ideological axe, nor impose any dogma unacceptable to scientists and disbelievers. The wonderful radiation of creative love by its living incarnations is acceptable to scientists and philosophers, to religious and moral leaders of different denominations, even to atheists and agnostics. It is the common ground and the common value for scientists, philosophers, religious leaders, irreligious sceptics, and for all, except perhaps the few partisans of hate, enmity, and evil who are still polluting the creative course of human history.

Besides the apostles of love, the moral guidance of scientific governments and ruled populations can successfully be discharged by the religious hierarchy and priesthood, if and when the official religious leaders neither distort the eternal moral precepts; nor misinterpret them; nor systematically transgress them in their thoughts, words, and actions; nor replace their cultivation by the much easier propagation of denominational rituals and ideologies. Up to the present time these deviations from the fulfillment of true spiritual and moral duties have been perpetrated now and then by leaders of practically all religions. In these periods of spiritual lassitude and moral fatigue, the fruitful moral influence of religious politicians naturally diminishes and sometimes turns into de-spiritualizing and demoralizing misguidance of rulers and ruled.

At the present time the body of religious leaders is undergoing a process of religious and moral polarization. Polarization has occurred regularly in catastrophic periods of practically all societies. In this sense it is one of the true uniformities in the sociocultural life of great and small societies.

The meaning of ethico-religious polarization is as follows: *in periods of catastrophe the majority of moral and religious leaders (and the general population also) who in normal times are neither too sinful nor too saintly, tend to split into extreme factions: some become more saintly, while some others become atheistic and demoralized "sinners."* The majority of normal times thus begins to shift more and more toward opposite poles of "sinners and saints."[7]

In the last few tragic decades this polarization has occurred among ethico-religious leaders, as well as in the whole human population. Among the

official religious authorities there can be observed a
growth and crystallization of religious politicians and
moral acrobats ranging from disguised atheists,
hypocrites, and cynics, to sterile ritualists, fanatics,
and morally indifferent executives and employees of
The Bigger and Better Religious Corporations.
Along with this negative polarization, a growth of
true religious and moral shepherds has also occurred.
While religious politicians can hardly exert a strong
creative influence upon governments and the public
at large, the true ethico-religious shepherds play an
important and lasting role in the moral guidance and
control of rulers and ruled.

Finally, a great moral influence has also been
exerted by the large groups of ordinary people who
just live a moral life in their daily living and relationships with their neighbors and the cosmos at
large. These unsung cultivators of morality and
spirituality neither pretend to lead anyone, nor claim
moral superiority over their fellow men. They are,
in fact, humble and self-critical. Many of them
practice moral self-control spontaneously and effort-
lessly, as their second nature. Without hesitation,
they take in stride all kinds of moral difficulties, solv-
ing them without violation of their moral convictions. Other good neighbors achieve moral self-control by strenuous effort, sometimes after suffering
several failures; nonetheless, they succeed in this difficult task of moral self-conversion and self-control.[8]

These grass-root cultivators of moral harvests
are the real social foundations of morality and spirituality. They can be found among practically all
communities and all denominations. Their propor-

tion varies from community to community, from period to period. But at all times, in all morally sound societies, they are the mainstay of moral order. They uphold it by their moral integrity, by living and practicing genuine moral values. A housewife who twice a week for years without any remuneration and incentive, works as a voluntary hospital nurse; carpenter, mason, doctor, or merchant who, again without any remuneration or social recognition, give their time, energy, or resources to the needy, are examples of these silent grass-root cultivators and builders of the moral Garden of Eden. As long as any society has among its members a substantial number of these mainstays of moral order, the social life of such societies remains free from excessive demoralization with its evil results.

Ascending governments of scientists of all nations, the United Nations, and the future World government can be enormously improved in their moral strength and wisdom by including in all governments these sages and moral experts. Their presence can prevent the governments from committing moral blunders, can increase their wisdom and morality and reinforce the total moral and spiritual order in the human universe.

Besides the moral guidance of governments from within, these creators, builders, and upholders of moral values can exert a decisive influence on humanity outside of government in their roles as: a) living examples of heroic morality; b) creators of new moral values; c) upholders of moral order; d) and as the most successful moral educators of themselves and the rest of mankind, through *free imitation* of their magnificent examples. If all these and other leaders and grass-root upholders of universal and immortal moral values are even loosely unified into a perfectly *free* World-Federation, their ethical influence can become decisive in preventing many catastrophes and uplifting mankind to a new and higher moral order in the human universe.

If *unification of the truly creative scientific, wise, and moral forces in all the governments and in mankind at large is supplemented by inclusion into the governments of the foremost creative artists of the fine arts (literature, drama, music, architecture, painting, sculpture), and by the cooperation of the creators of Beauty with those of Truth and Goodness outside the governments, such a Union of the creators of the greatest values of Truth, Goodness, and Beauty on this planet would give to mankind the best possible government and social order.* An actual membership in any government of the foremost artists, like Bach or Beethoven, Phidias or Michelangelo, Rafael or Leonardo, Dante or Shakespeare, can greatly contribute to its creativity, enrich it by intuitional wisdom, purify it of vulgar ugliness, and ennoble its "body and soul" by radiation of immortal beauty.

The greatest possible defects of the hitherto existing Sensate governments have been exactly the separation of these supreme values and their creators from each other in the system of values, activities, and in the personnel of the governments — an insignificant role given to the cultivation of these values, and to their creators in the policies and membership of the governments. The governments of

Sensate politicians have rarely had among their high ranks even a small number of the foremost creators of Truth, Goodness, and Beauty. Sensate governments of this sort have consisted mainly of persons who have neither creative potential nor a discriminating appreciation of these supreme values. Specifically, the talents of most of the ruling politicians have consisted of: a skill in machinations and manipulations of mainly low-grade human emotions and interrelationships; the art of making money by all available means; unscrupulous use of naked force for promotion of their ambitions; an elastic conscience which easily excuses crimes committed by politicians, and a talent for diplomatic hypocrisy, sincere lying, cruelty, and insensitivity far exceeding that of the ruled in these political maneuvers.

In accordance with this, an overwhelming majority of the existing governments of Sensate politicians have been Machiavellian in nature. Of all the important groups (e.g. family, religious, scientific, ethical, and other organizations), the state has been the most Machiavellian and cynical in its policy of *raison d'etat,* in its power politics, and in its application of the rule that might is right. Its representatives are the eminently perfidious and nihilistic embodiments of naked power politics. No matter how noble they may be in their private capacities, when they act as state-agents they largely become the instruments of rude force assisted by fraud. Machiavelli undoubtedly exaggerated these unseemly aspects of the Sensate rulers, but he correctly pointed out these most important characteristics of Sensate politicians.

CHAPTER XII

FROM SENSATE GOVERNMENT
TO INTEGRAL LEADERSHIP

If the total Western sociocultural world is pass-ing now from the disintegrating Sensate order to a new Integral one; and if in this passage mankind does not commit suicide, the hitherto dominant Sen-sate governments of politicians are bound to give place to the new Integral type of government.

This trend has already begun and, if mankind can avoid a new world-war, it is bound to develop as part of a much more general trend in which the hitherto dominant Sensate sociocultural order will be replaced by the new Integral system of culture and social organization. The outlined government con-sisting of: a) scientists of the natural, social, and humanistic disciplines; b) sages and wise men; c) moral and spiritual leaders; and d) foremost mas-ters and creators in the fine arts, is the type of gov-ernment that meets the requirements of the new Integral culture.

For the hard-headed and thick-headed Sensate politicians and ideologists, the preceding portrait of Sensate governments of politicians may appear as an ugly caricature of the Sensate original, while the portraits of Integral government may impress them as an idealized and beautified picture of wishful but unrealistic fiction. These politicians and ideologists are bound to be still more skeptical in regard to the outlined trend of the replacement of the Sensate by Integral government. Hardly any one can joyfully welcome his own social and political death; and such a welcome can least be expected from the ruling Sensate politicians. Because of their vested interests, the Sensate governments and their ideologists can only reject the above propositions as invalid and utopian.

All such criticisms and objections can be easily answered. To the criticism that the above portrait of the Sensate governments of politicians is a distorted caricature of the original, we respectfully submit that our portrait of the Sensate Ruling groups is much more flattering than the Machiavellian portrait which practically all Sensate ideologists and political scientists have been accepting and extolling as perfectly realistic and scientific. If this be so, then our portrait cannot be a dirtied distortion of the original because it depicts Sensate rulers as being much less vicious, cynical, cruel, bestial, tyrannical, and criminal than they are as portrayed by Machiavelli.

We can add to this that our portrait outlines the governments of politicians at the decaying stage of the Sensate sociocultural order generally and the Sensate political regime specifically. During the ascending stage of the Sensate cultural system, the Sensate governments of politicians were more creative and more beneficial to their nations and in-groups than they are during their declining stage.

As to the objection that the sketched Integral government is a mere wishful fiction unrealizable in actual social life, it may be replied that in an imperfect form this type of government has been realized many times in past history. There is no strong reason why in an ennobled form it cannot again be established in the near future. We have seen that the emergence of a new Integral government has already begun.

The objection that only the cynical Machiavellian government of naked force, terror, and fraud can be effective and that none of the too moral, too wise, too aesthetic, and too scientific governments can efficaciously control the unruly millions is grossly incorrect. First, Machiavelli's own experience decisively repudiated his early theories of this sort. As is well known, his ideology was inspired by the cynical, bestial, coercive, murderous, amoral, and irreligious policies of Cesare Borgia (1476-1507). In this irreligious Cardinal, bastard-Prince and utterly unscrupulous ruler, Machiavelli hoped to see the unifying savior of Italy and the architect-builder of a stable and peaceful social order in the chaotic age of the Italian Renaissance. During his own lifetime, Machiavelli witnessed and conceded a complete repudiation of his supposedly bluntly realistic theories by the historical facts: Cesare's policy brought only a catastrophic destruction of many cities and principalities of Italy; death of thousands of victims of Cesare's aggressive wars; torture, suffering, and the death of dozens, possibly even of hundreds of Cesare's personal victims including several of his closest relatives; his cynical violation of all divine and human laws, perpetration of all the most horrible crimes; and, finally, the overthrow, imprisonment, and inglorious death of Cesare Borgia himself. These facts were a categorical repudiation of Machiavelli's theories regarding the effectiveness of government by force and fraud.

Mainly destructive results have been also caused by similar policies of murder, force, and fraud of Marius or Sulla, Genghis Khan or Tamerlane, Hitler or Stalin, to mention but a few names out of many tyrannical rulers and conquerors of the past.

As a general rule, the empires and organizations built mainly by rude force, fraud, bloody strife, and violation of the universal moral imperatives have been short-lived and disastrous. The empires built by Alexander the Great and Hannibal, by Pompei and Attila, by Genghis Khan and Tamerlane, by Napoleon and Hitler, are examples of such short-lived organizations. Moderate also has been the life-span of organizations built by moderately selfish economic interests. The average life-span of small business organizations like drug or hardware stores is only about four years, while the average life-span of the big business firms listed on the stock market is only 29 years. The longest existing organizations have been those animated by spiritual and altruistic forces for realization of the supreme values of God, Truth, Goodness, and Beauty. Such are the great ethico-religious organizations. The Taoist, Confucianist, Hindu, Buddhist, Jainist, Judaist, Christian, Mohammedan, and other religious and ethical organizations have already lived one, two, or three millennia; and so far they do not show any clear sign of irretrievable disintegration.[1]

This means that the really fruitful and constructive policy of any government-builder, anxious to build a durable organization, is that of scientifically-competent and wise realization of the moral values of love, friendship, mutual help and compassion, and not the policy motivated by unlimited egoism, hate and nihilism and carried on by coercion, fraud, hypocrisy and other anti-moral and ugly means.

In accordance with the ancient verity that God is Love and Love, not hate, is the creative genius of history, contemporary biology, psychology, and sociology recognize unanimously the decisive role of mutual aid, cooperation, friendship, and unselfish creative love in biological evolution of species and especially in the creative achievements of mankind. The role of this factor has been more important than that of the struggle for existence.[2]   Only those governments and ruling activities which have been moved by charitable, friendly, cooperative moral forces (plus, of course, the forces of wisdom, science, and beauty) have been really constructive. As a rule, it is the Machiavellian governments which create anarchy and disaster as a result of their policies, and it is the Integral governments which liquidate this anarchy and disaster, cure the wounds, establish order, and revive the creative progress of their societies.

As in biological illness, violence and blind bloodshed cannot effect the cure of social sickness. Scientific competence and sincere love for the patient are no less necessary here than in medical illness. If even a social operation is in order, it must be a competent surgical operation, not blind butchery. It must be aimed at curing the patient, and not at killing him; working through peaceful and orderly therapy, not violent and destructive bloodshed. These conditions explain why social reconstructions, animated by sincere sympathy, competently planned and systematically carried on, turn out to be more successful in curing social sickness and improving the well-being of society than hate-inspired wars and revolutions. In social as well as medical operations, hate-laden butchery kills rather than revives. If something good comes of such wars and revolutions, it is due to a current (however small) of unselfish love and disinterested desire to help the suffering multitudes frequently present in these upheavals.

Of course in addition, most of the positive results of such violent movements are obtained through the spoiling of other groups, at the cost of their suffering, and often their very lives. Most of the achievements of wars and revolutions are merely the plundering of the defeated by the victorious. Transference of goods from one ruling gang to another does not enrich the whole society, nor does it increase the total sum of the goods. It does not eliminate mutual hates, antagonisms, and injustices, nor does it cure the social sickness. It merely changes the ruling actors and the forms of tyranny, exploitation, misery, injustice, hate, and tensions without notably decreasing the total fund of social evils.

While the victorious ruling faction profits by war or violent revolution, the populations of both struggling parties must bear the cost. And the bloodier the struggle, the greater the cost in life, property, and happiness for the masses. In protracted and bloody struggles, the vital, economic, mental, and moral losses of the vast strata of both parties ordinarily far exceed their gains. While the small ruling groups — of Genghis Khan or Napoleon, of Marius or Sulla, of Caesar or Anthony, of Cromwell or Robespierre, of Lenin or Hitler — for a short time profited enormously by their victories, the vast multitudes of their peoples were about ruined by the struggle. Sometimes the ruin was irreparable and eventually led to the decline of the bled nations and their cultural creativity. Bloody civil strifes and the Peloponnesian war ushered in the decay of Greece; the costly wars and civil struggles of Marius and Sulla, of the First and Second Triumvirate started the decline of the Roman Empire. The bloodshed of the French Revolution and of the Napoleonic wars prepared the subsequent eclipse of France. The same can be said of the wars of Suleiman the Magnificent in regard to the Turkish Empire, or of the decay of the Old Kingdom, of the Middle and the New Empire in Egypt. Finally, the bloodiest revolutions and the World Wars of our time have brought the whole of mankind, especially the belligerent and turbulent West (including Russia) to the brink of an apocalyptic catastrophe. Only wisely and scientifically guided forces of love and free cooperation can perform the constructive functions. Where they are lacking, no constructive results for humanity can be expected.

A vast body of factual and logical evidence well supports these conclusions. Among other things, they mean that the fashionable Machiavellian theories of the government of force and fraud as the only effective government are fallacious. This sort of policy appears to be the most unrealistic and hopeless policy for prevention and elimination of war, anarchy, and destruction, and for building a harmonious and peaceful order in the total human universe. The contemporary rulers and politicians who sincerely believe in and practice this carnivorous policy for realization of noble purposes are ignorant, unrealistic, and the most dangerous leaders of nations and of humanity at large. Unfortunately, most of today's governments do believe in, and do follow this predatory policy. Their slogans are familiar: peace "through power," "through massive retaliation," "through more terrible and destructive arms," even through being first in the deadly blow that will murder millions of innocent people; these slogans and preparations show clearly their adherence to Machiavellian principles. These rulers seem to be still ignorant of the well-tested verities that hate generates hate and love begets love; that aggression and fraud breed aggression and fraud; and that a policy of war is answered by war.

Instead of these verities, our politicians seem to believe that war is the best way to peace, hatred to love, and fraud to sincerity; that murder and harm are the best remedies for health and life. No wonder that their efforts have made the twentieth century the bloodiest, most inhuman, most destructive, and the least peaceful of all the preceding twenty-five. No wonder that they have succeeded well in bringing mankind not only to the brink of a new world-war, but to the brink of its death, and the end of its creative history. It is indeed hard to find more unrealistic, impractical, and dangerous leaders of mankind than the contemporary Sensate politicians of force, fraud, death, and destruction! There is no strong reason to expect from these governments either establishment of lasting peace or of a harmonious order with security, dignity, and freedom

for all. Still less can today's governments of politicians be entrusted with the life, fortunes, and
future of the human race. A successful solution of
the tremendously difficult tasks of our time is obvi-
ously far beyond their capacity and ability. They
can solve some of these tasks only with the help of
all the creative forces of mankind, and only if and
when these governments can transform their Sensate-
Machiavellian soul into an Integral one. Otherwise, they should be replaced in an orderly way by
the new Integral governments of scientists, sages,
moral, spiritual, and aesthetic leaders. Such a transformation or replacement is required by the supreme
goals of the survival, well-being, and creative renaissance of humanity.

Mankind's situation today is too critical to
attempt a cure by superficial, partly doubtful, and
partly wrong measures. Mankind is now at the
stormiest point in its passage from the disintegrating
Sensate culture, values, social institutions, government, and type of personality, to the emerging
Integral, Familistic, social, cultural, and personal
order. For crossing the first part of this passage,
humanity has already paid a tremendously high
price — the price of two World Wars, and many
smaller wars and bloody revolts, with millions of
human lives lost, a vast part of the inhabited earth
ruined, an unbounded ocean of sorrow suffered by
hundreds of millions. These tremendous losses have
greatly weakened mankind. At its middle point, it
is now confronted with an additional deadly danger
— the suicidal threat of a thermo-nuclear war.
Under such tragic conditions, mankind can reach
the sought-after haven only by mobilizing all its

creative forces. The aroused and unified forces can guide the dangerous passage more safely, and with less bloodshed than the declining governments of Sensate politicians. If present and future governments are deprived (through the universal and total disarmament) of the legal and the factual possibility of starting a new war, this radical limitation of their power will force the governments to improve morally and prevent them from plunging mankind into an apocalyptic war. If through these measures we are given a few decades of peace, during this period of respite, under the guidance of the unified creative forces, the most dangerous part of the passage can be accomplished and a solid foundation for the emerging Integral order built. The establishment of the new order means the magnificent era of man's creative history.

FOOTNOTES

CHAPTER ONE FOOTNOTES

[1]See a development of these views and their history in Benedetto Croce, *Politics and Morals,* tr. S. J. Castiglione, New York, 1945, pp. 3, 4, 60, 65, *et passim.*

[2]N. Machiavelli, *The Prince,* A Mentor Book, New York, The New American Library of World Literature, 1957, pp. 92-93, 98-103.

[3]Cf. P. Sorokin, *Crisis of Our Age,* New York, E. P. Dutton & Co., 1957, ch. IV; P. Sorokin, *Social and Cultural Dynamics,* Boston, Porter Sargent, 1957, ch. 24, 25.

[4]Lord Acton, *Essays on Freedom and Power,* Boston, Beacon Press, 1948, pp. 364, 370.

[5]See the detailed study of the criminal codes from this standpoint in P. Sorokin, *Social and Cultural Dynamics,* four-volume edition, New York, American Book Co., 1937-41, vol. III, ch. 13-15.

[6]Narada, I:1, 2; Brihaspati, I:1, in *The Sacred Books of the East,* vol. XXXIII, Oxford, 1889.

[7]The Laws of Manu, VII:14-22, *Ibid.,* vol. XXV, Oxford, 1886.

[8]Gautama, XI: 1-7; Apastamba, II:10, 25; *Sacred Books of the East,* vol. II, Oxford, 1879.

[9]*The Sacred Books of the Hindus,* vol. XVI, Allahabad, 1914, p. 40.

[10]Gautama, XII:48.

[11]Tao-Teh-King, 6; in *The Sacred Books of the East,* vol. XL, Oxford, 1891.

[12]*Ibid.,* pp. 251-52.

[13]*Ibid.,* pp. 3-4.

[14]Lao-Tse's Canon of Reason and Virtue, 9, in W. S. A. Pott, tr., *Chinese Political Philosophy,* New York, 1925, p. 106.

[15]Various condemnatory views in regard to either all forms of government or to most of them have been expressed by many thinkers like Plato (in regard to timocracy, oligarchy, tyranny, democracy, with the exception of the government of the sages-philosophers), Aristotle (in regard to oligarchic, tyrannical, and mob-rule governments), by Polybius, Cicero, some of the Cynics, the Stoics and the Epicureans, by several Church-Fathers, and Mediaeval ideologists, by many a Hindu, Jainist, Buddhist, Sufist, and the Western thinkers of the later centuries up to the present time. Of various currents of political thought the ideologists of Anarchism, from W. Godwin to Bakunin, Kropotkin, and others, leaders of several religious sects and pacifist groups up to the mutual — vituperative — criticism of each government or political party by its opponents and adversaries have been continuously active in their condemnation of moral misbehavior of either all or some of the governments and rulers.

[16]H. Spencer, *Principles of Sociology,* vol. I, London, 1885, pp. 545-52.

[17]Cf. H. Spencer, The Principles of Ethics, par. 364, See especially his *The Man vs. State.*

[18]P. Kropotkin, *Mutual Aid,* Boston, Extending Horizons Press, 1955, p. 216.

[19]Leo Tolstoy, *The Kingdom of God is Within You,* Cassel Co., 1894, pp. 102, 167.

[20]G. Maximoff, ed., *The Political Philosophy of Bakunin,* Glencoe, Free Press, 1953, p. 248.

[21]Lord Acton, *Essays on Freedom and Power, op. cit.,* pp. 364, 370.

CHAPTER TWO FOOTNOTES

[1]F. Dostoievski, *Zapiski is mertvago doma* (House of The Dead).

[2]P. Sorokin, *Social Mobility,* Glencoe, Free Press, 1959, pp. 300-311. P. Sorokin, *Sociology of Revolution,* Philadelphia, Lippincott, 1925.

[3]Cf. Norwood East, *Society and the Criminal,* H.M.S.O., 1949; Alex Comfort, *Authority and Delinquency in the Modern State,* London, 1950, ch. 2; C. S. Bluemel, *War, Politics, and Insanity,* Denver, The World Press, 1950, ch. 1, 8, 9; G. Mosca, *The Ruling Class,* New York, McGraw-Hill, 1939, pp. 122ff., 401ff.

[4]Aggressiveness, and an obsessive-compulsive reaction, combined with mania or paranoia, or schizophrenia or melancholia, or psychopathic state seem to be most frequent types of mental (and moral) disorders among rulers. Aggressiveness and obsessive-compulsive complex, combined now with mania and hypermania, now with paranoia, now with schizophrenia or melancholia or psychopathic state or senile dementia seem to be the most frequent types of mental (and moral) disorders among the ruling groups. Cf. the quoted works of N. East, A. Comfort, C. S. Bluemel, G. Mosca.

[5]Cf. the details in P. Sorokin, "Monarchs and Rulers: A Comparative Statistical Study," *Social Forces,* vol. IV, 1925, pp. 525-26.

[6]See about the law of mental, moral, and religious polarization in catastrophic, chaotic, and self-contradictory conditions in P. Sorokin, *Man and Society in Calamity,* New York, E. P. Dutton & Co., 1943, ch. 9-14; and in P. Sorokin, *The Ways and Power of Love,* Boston, 1958, ch. 12.

CHAPTER THREE FOOTNOTES

[1]Diehl, Charles, *Byzantium: Greatness and Decline,* Rutgers University Press, 1957, pp. 128, 136.

[2]When the Senators, disturbed by the cries of the massacred victims, wanted to know the cause of these cries, Sulla coldly said: *"Agamus, patres conscripti, seditiosi pauculi meo issu occiduntur* (let us proceed, senators; it is only a few seditious persons are being killed by my orders)." The number of these "seditious few" was some 8,000 to 10,000.

[3]Taken from P. Sorokin, "Monarchs and Rulers: Comparative Study," *Social Forces,* vol. IV, pp. 524-25.

[4]The rates for 1956 are for 100 persons of 80,986,991 population in 2,640 cities and converted from data in *Uniform Crime Reports,* F.B.I., U. S. Dept. of Justice, Washington, D. C., for respective years.

[5]See H. Zink, *City Bosses in The United States,* Duke University Press, 1930; David Loth, *Public Plunder: A History of Graft in America,* New York, 1938.

[6]See the details in David Loth, *Public Plunder: A History of Graft in America, op. cit.*, G. Graham, *Morality in American Politics,* New York, 1952.

CHAPTER FOUR FOOTNOTES

[1]See for the United States: G. Myers, *History of the Great American Fortunes,* New York, 1936; Dixon Wecter, *The Saga of American Society,* New York, 1937; M. Josephson, *The Robber Barons,* New York, 1934; F. L. Allen, *The Lords of Creation,* New York, 1935; F. Lundberg, *America's 60 Families,* New York, 1937; W. Miller (ed), *Men in Business,* Cambridge, 1952; C. Wright Mills, *The Power Elite,* New York, 1956. See other sources and literature in these works.

[2]See A. R. Barrett, *The Era of Fraud and Embezzlement,* Boston, 1895.

[3]R. T. Wood, *Millions Under Bond,* American Surety Co.; J. Hall, *Theft, Law and Society,* Indianapolis, 1952.

[4]These cases are reported in the N. Y. *Times,* Sept. 6, 1913; Feb. 4, 1931; Feb. 28, 1931; May 6, 1931; Sept. 2, 1931; Chicago *Tribune,* Sept. 26, 1934; Indianapolis *Star,* June 30, 1939; see other cases in Wood's referred work.

[5]F. Lundberg, *America's 60 Families, op. cit.,* p. 201.
[6]See H. Zink, *City Bosses in the United States,* Duke University Press, 1930; D. Loth, *Public Plunder,* New York, 1938; New York City Board of Aldermen, *Special Committee to Investigate the Ring Frauds,* New York, 1878.

[7]See the details and other cases in reports of the Kefauver hearings, particularly in the *Third Interim Report of the Special Committee to Investigate Organized Crime in Interstate Commerce,* 82nd Congress, 1st Session, Report 307; A. R. Lindesmith, "Organized Crime," *Annals of American Academy of Political and Social Science,* September, 1941; C. Wright Mills, *The Power Elite, op. cit.,* ch. 14, 15.

CHAPTER FIVE FOOTNOTES

[1]See the detailed investigation of all wars and all significant internal revolutions from 600 B.C. up to the present time in P. Sorokin, *Social and Cultural Dynamics, op. cit.,* vol. III, pp. 259-508; in abridged, one-volume edition of this work, ch. 32-35.

CHAPTER SIX FOOTNOTES

[1]Cf. a detailed study of all the wars and important internal disturbances in these countries from 600 B.C. up to the present time in P. A. Sorokin, *Social and Cultural Dynamics, op. cit.,* vol. III, or ch. 32-35 in abridged one-volume edition of this work.

[2]See about the nature of the crisis of our times and the totalitarian effects of great emergencies, like famine, depression, war, revolution, epidemics, etc., upon social and political regimes, in P. Sorokin, *Crisis of Our Age;* P. Sorokin, *Social and Cultural Dynamics,* abridged one-volume edition; and P. Sorokin, *Man and Society in Calamity.*

[3]Cf. P. Sorokin's *Social and Cultural Dynamics, Crisis of Our Age, Reconstruction of Humanity,* and *The Ways and Power of Love.*

CHAPTER SEVEN FOOTNOTES

[1]Its blueprint is given in P. Sorokin, *Reconstruction of Humanity,* and *The Ways and Power of Love.*

[2]Cf. on these techniques and methods: P. Sorokin, *The Ways and Power of Love,* and P. Sorokin (ed.), *Symposium: Forms and Techniques of Altruistic and Spiritual Growth,* Boston, Beacon Press, 1954.

CHAPTER EIGHT FOOTNOTES

[1]See P. Sorokin, *Social and Cultural Dynamics,* and *Crisis of Our Age, S.O.S.: The Meaning of Our Crisis,* Boston, Beacon Press, 1951.

[2]*Crisis of Our Age,* p. 13.

[3]Cf. for development and coroboration of this: P. Sorokin, *The Ways and Power of Love,* ch. 5-6; in *Dynamics,* v. IV, ch. 16; in *Dynamics* abridged edition, ch. 41.

[4]Cf. P. Kropotkin, *Mutual Aid,* Boston, Porter Sargent, 1955; A. Montagu, *On Being Human,* New York, H. Schuman, 1950; P. Sorokin, *The Ways and Power of Love.*

[5]Cf. for the evidence, P. Sorokin, *The Ways and Power of Love,* ch. 4, *et passim.*

[6]Cf. P. Sorokin, *Fads and Foibles in Modern Sociology and Related Sciences,* Chicago, H. Regnery, 1956.

[7]Cf. P. Sorokin, *Dynamics,* ch. 5-12; P. Sorokin, *The American Sex Revolution,* Boston, Porter Sargent, 1957.

CHAPTER NINE FOOTNOTES

[1]Cf. for detailed analysis of these relationships and their fluctuation: P. Sorokin, *Dynamics,* abridged edition, ch. 26-31; P. Sorokin, *Crisis of Our Age,* ch. V.

[2]Cf. for analysis of these reasons: *Dynamics* and *The Crisis of Our Age.*

[3]Cf. P. Sorokin, *The American Sex Revolution.*

[4]See evidence and data in P. Sorokin, *Dynamics,* v. III; in abridged edition, ch. 32-35.

[5]P. Sorokin, *Crisis of Our Age,* p. 194.

[6]*Ibid.,* p. 203. See there a detailed analysis of this imminent degeneration of contractual relationship and Sensate order itself.

CHAPTER TEN FOOTNOTES

[1]Cf. Aristotle, *The Nichomachean Ethics,* bks. VIII and IX., 1166a; "The friends are strong in the strength, rich in the opulence, and powerful in the power of each other." Cicero, *On Friendship,* Everyman's Library Edition, p. 179.

[2]P. Sorokin, *Society, Culture and Personality,* New York, Harpers, 1947, p. 100.

[3]See on this P. Kropotkin, *Mutual Aid, op. cit.* Cf. for other up-to-date literature on this problem A. Montagu's quoted work.

[4]P. Sorokin, *Studies of the Harvard Research Center in Creative Altruism,* p. 3. For the evidence confirming these statements, see P. Sorokin, *The Ways and Power of Love,* ch. 4 *et passim.* P. Sorokin, *Forms and Techniques of Altruistic and Spiritual Growth,* Boston, Beacon Press, 1954.

[5]P. Sorokin, *The Ways and Power of Love,* pp. 464ff.

CHAPTER ELEVEN FOOTNOTES

[1]P. Sorokin, *Reconstruction of Humanity*, p. 74. Cf. also C. F. Chassell, *The Relationship Between Morality and Intellect*, New York, Columbia University Press, 1935.

[2]For the sources of these figures and indexes see P. Sorokin, *Social and Cultural Dynamics*, vol. II, ch. 3 and vol. III, ch. 9-14; or ch. 13, 14, 32-35 in abridged, one-volume edition of this work; W. A. Lunden, *The Dynamics of Higher Education*, Pittsburgh, Pittsburg Printing Co., 1939, ch. 15.

[3]See a detailed analysis of ethical systems and the criminal codes from this standpoint in P. Sorokin, *Social and Cultural Dynamics*, vol. II, ch. 13, 14, 15; in the abridged edition of this work, ch. 24, 25.

[4]See on this P. Sorokin, *The Ways and Power of Love;* P. Sorokin (ed.), *Forms and Techniques of Altruistic and Spiritual Growth;* and P. Sorokin, *Studies of Harvard Research Center in Creative Altruism.*

[5]Cf. on this *Dynamics*, vol. III, ch. 5; in the abridged edition, ch. 28.

[6]P. Sorokin, *The Ways and Power of Love*, p. 71.

[7]Cf. about this "law of polarization" in catastrophes and frustrations: P. Sorokin, *Man and Society in Calamity*, New York, E. P. Dutton & Co., 1943, ch. 9-12; P. Sorokin, *The Ways and Power of Love*, ch. 12; For the law of polarization among prisoners of war, see W. A. Lunden, "The Crucible of Captivity," *The Deltan*, Vol. XXVII, No. 3, 1957, pp. 4-14.

[8]Cf. on these two types: "the fortunate" and "catastrophic" altruists: P. Sorokin, *The Ways and Power of Love*, ch. 9, 12.

CHAPTER TWELVE FOOTNOTES

[1]See on the life-span of various organizations: P. Sorokin, *Society, Culture and Personality*, New York, Harper's, 1947, ch. 34.

[2]Cf. on this: P. Sorokin (ed.), *Exploration in Altruistic Love and Behavior: Symposium*, Boston, Beacon Press, 1950; P. Sorokin (ed.), *Forms and Techniques of Altruistic and Spiritual Growth: Symposium;* P. Sorokin, *The Ways and Power of Love.*

BRIEF SUBJECT INDEX

BRIEF SUBJECT INDEX — *Continued*

OTHER EXTENDING
HORIZONS BOOKS

THE AMERICAN SEX REVOLUTION

by Pitirim Sorokin
186 pp, $3.50 cloth, $2.00 paper

An eminent Harvard sociologist takes a long and critical look at the sexual attitudes and habits of American men and women. Honestly and courageously he condemns "loose behavior and false values," and warns that our world leadership is threatened by the possibility of complete sex anarchy.

THE INTEGRATION OF HUMAN KNOWLEDGE
by Oliver L. Reiser
478 pp, $8.00

In his quest for a universal ethic, Dr. Reiser presents a philosophy for Scientific Humanism that is at once challenging, controversial and creative. He advocates a synthesis of science and philosophy and a re-evaluation of man's knowledge of himself and the sciences.

MARRIAGE PAST AND PRESENT

A Debate between Bronislaw Malinowski and Robert Briffault
96 pp, cloth $2.50, paper $1.50

Two famous anthropologists debate the nature and prospects of marriage in Western civilization. E.F. Ashley Montagu has contributed an illuminating introduction and invaluable textual notes.

MUTUAL AID

by Petr Kropotkin
326 + xxxviii pp.
$3.00 cloth, $2.00 paper

Long out of print, and long in demand, "Mutual Aid" is now issued in a special edition, with Foreword and Bibliography, and including for the first time in any publication of the book the essay "The Struggle for Existence" by T.H. Huxley, to which it is a detailed reply.

SOCIAL AND CULTURAL DYNAMICS
721 pp, $7.50

A study of change in major systems of art, truth, ethics, law and social relationships, this one-volume "abridgement" of Pitirim Sorokin's four-volume masterpiece, revised and abridged by the author for the general reading public, makes available in easily understandable language a monumental sociological study.

OTHER EXTENDING
HORIZONS BOOKS

TOYNBEE AND HISTORY

ed. by M.F. Ashley Montagu
400 pp, $5.00

In this volume edited by Mr. Montagu, some thirty experts in the various fields with which Toynbee deals have been brought together and examine precisely what the nature of Toynbee's contribution has been.

ANTHROPOLOGY AND HUMAN NATURE

by M.F. Ashley Montagu
390 pp, $6.00

Professor Montagu gives to his book the frank, open viewpoint of modern anthropology "cutting across the boundaries which separate the sciences from the humanities, while embracing both."